30 New Zealand Stories for Children

30 New Zealand Stories for Children

Edited by **Jo Noble**
Illustrations by **David Elliot**

RANDOM HOUSE
NEW ZEALAND

The publishers would like to acknowledge the Dunedin College of Education Children's Writing Fellowship which allowed David Elliot to complete the illustrations.

A RANDOM HOUSE BOOK
published by
Random House New Zealand
18 Poland Road, Glenfield, Auckland, New Zealand
www.randomhouse.co.nz

First published 2000, reprinted 2000, 2001

ISBN 1 86941 437 3

Cover image inspired by 'Sebastian' written by Janice Leitch
Cover illustration: David Elliot
Printed in China

Contents

	Foreword	7
	Acknowledgements	8
1.	The Reading Room Joy Cowley	9
2.	Pavlova Queen Rose Hudson	11
3.	Trapped by an Octopus Janet Slater Bottin	14
4.	Witches Britches Karen Sidney	17
5.	Silent Reading David Hill	21
6.	The Super-Trolley Cynthia Todd Maguire	24
7.	Uncle Trev and the Light Bulb Jack Lasenby	28
8.	Circus Routine Diana Noonan	33
9.	Roimata and the Forest of Tane Miriam Smith	38
10.	The Case of the Phantom Tagger Margaret Schroder	42
11.	Mayday! Christine Ashton	45
12.	Green Marmalade to You Margaret Mahy	50
13.	Parent Help? Anna Kenna	52
14.	Leila's Lunch Jane Buxton	57
15.	Weapons of Mass Description Anna Kenna	60
16.	The Violin Gillian S. Findsen	66
17.	A Load of Junk John Lockyer	70
18.	Horse Adrienne Jansen	73
19.	Uncle Trev and the Howling Dog Service Jack Lasenby	77
20.	Would You Like to be a Parrot? Barbara Hill	82
21.	The Caves in the Cliff Patricia Irene Johnson	87
22.	The Chocolate Bomb Stuart Payne	92
23.	Ms Winsley and the Pirate Who Didn't Have a Problem Barbara Else	96
24.	Intruders Elizabeth Best	101
25.	Why Anna Hung Upside Down Margaret Mahy	106
26.	Beans Patricia Grace	110
27.	When Mum Won Lotto Valerie Batchelor	114
28.	Sebastian Janice Leitch	116
29.	Just One Thing K.E. Anderson	119
30.	Where's Pete? Penelope Newman	122
	Index	125

Foreword

It's time for a story . . .

Any time is time for a story — time to imagine yourself into somebody else's shoes, feel what they're feeling, be happy with them, or sad, scared or safe, maybe a little puzzled.

We've selected the stories in this book so you'll experience some of all these things. Most of them are funny or happy, although a few are not. They are all written by New Zealand writers, many are set in our country but some could be set anywhere in the world. That's what makes stories so special — they take you, in your imagination, to places real and fancied, on journeys and adventures you may never be able to experience in real life.

These stories are fairly short so they can be read (or listened to) in a short space of time. Maybe you can share them with somebody in your family, with friends, or perhaps your teacher will read them to your class.

You might even find a place where you can sneak off and read when you should be somewhere else or doing something else — like Joy Cowley's bookworm in the first story in the collection.

There's a story in everything around you, if you look for it. That's what the writers of these stories have done — they have brought back a memory or spelled out a dream; they have thought of something, turned it on its head, twisted it round and asked themselves, "What if?" And it has turned into a story.

You'll find a favourite somewhere here, a story that triggers a happy response or makes you think, you'll find a smile in most of the stories and I know you'll chortle at David Elliot's clever illustrations.

Happy reading!

Jo Noble
July 2000

Acknowledgements

The publishers gratefully acknowledge the following authors, publishers, literary agencies and copyright holders for permission to reproduce the stories. (LML), SJ = Learning Media Ltd, *School Journal*.

1. 'The Reading Room', © Joy Cowley, (LML), *SJ*:3:1, 1996.
2. 'Pavlova Queen', © Rose Hudson, (LML), *SJ*:2:2, 1997.
3. 'Trapped by an Octopus', © Janet Slater Bottin, (LML), *SJ*:1:2, 1996.
4. 'Witches Britches', © Karen Sidney, *Te Ao Marama*, Ed. Witi Ihimaera, Vol IV, *Te Ara o Te Hau*, Reed, 1994.
5. 'Silent Reading', © David Hill, (LML), *SJ*:2:2, 1999.
6. 'The Super-Trolley', © Cynthia Todd Maguire, *The Ears Storybook*, Random Century, 1991.
7. 'Uncle Trev and the Light Bulb', © Jack Lasenby, *Uncle Trev*, Cape Catley, 1991.
8. 'Circus Routine', © Diana Noonan, (LML), *SJ*:3:3, 1996.
9. 'Roimata and the Forest of Tane', © Miriam Smith, *The Ears Storybook*, Random Century, 1991.*
10. 'The Case of the Phantom Tagger', © Margaret Schroder, (LML), *SJ*:4:1, 1998.
11. 'Mayday!', © Christine Ashton, (LML), *SJ*:3:2, 1996.
12. 'Green Marmalade to You', © Margaret Mahy, *Nonstop Nonsense*, J.M. Dent, 1996.
13. 'Parent Help?', © Anna Kenna, (LML), *SJ*:3:2, 1999.
14. 'Leila's Lunch', © Jane Buxton, (LML), *SJ*:1:4, 1996.
15. 'Weapons of Mass Description', © Anna Kenna, (LML), *SJ*:3:1, 1999.
16. 'The Violin', © Gillian S. Findsen, *Allsorts,* October 1997.
17. 'A Load of Junk', © John Lockyer, (LML), *SJ*:1:4, 1998.
18. 'Horse', © Adrienne Jansen, (LML), *SJ*:2:4, 1994.
19. 'Uncle Trev and the Howling Dog Service', © Jack Lasenby, *Uncle Trev*, Cape Catley, 1991.
20. 'Would You Like to be a Parrot?' © Barbara Hill, *The Ears Storybook*, Random Century, 1991.
21. 'The Caves in the Cliff' © Patricia Irene Johnson, *Allsorts,* December 1997.*
22. 'The Chocolate Bomb', © Stuart Payne, *Allsorts,* January 1997.
23. 'Ms Winsley and the Pirate Who Didn't Have a Problem' © Barbara Else, *Tricky Situations*, Godwit, 1999.
24. 'Intruders', © Elizabeth Best, (LML), *SJ*:3:3, 1999.
25. 'Why Anna Hung Upside Down', © Margaret Mahy, *Nonstop Nonsense*, J.M. Dent, 1996.
26. 'Beans', © Patricia Grace, *E Ao Marama*, Ed. Witi Ihimaera, Vol IV, *Te Ara o Te Hau*, Reed, 1994.
27. 'When Mum Won Lotto', © Valerie Batchelor, (LML), *SJ*:1:1, 1998.
28. 'Sebastian', © Janice Leitch, *Allsorts*, March 1998.
29. 'Just One Thing', © K.E. Anderson, (LML), *SJ*:2:1, 1998.
30. 'Where's Pete?', © Penelope Newman, (LML), *SJ*:1:4, 1999.

* Every effort was made to contact these authors but without success.

The Reading Room

Joy Cowley

Oh, no—Mum's finished on the telephone. Any minute now she'll be finding a job for me. I sneak out of the kitchen and down the hall. I lock the door and put the seat down. I *have* to finish this book. It's about a boy called Mark who gets lost in a snowstorm. If someone doesn't find him, he'll die.

My sister Kathy bangs on the door. "Lisa!" she yells. "Hurry up in there."

"I won't be long," I tell her.

Mark can't see anything through the whirling snowflakes. His hands are numb. His feet feel like ice. Suddenly, he slips and falls over a cliff. Oh, no!

"Lisa!" calls Kathy. "I have to have a shower!"

Mark lands on a ledge. Thank goodness for that! But he thinks his leg is broken. He is in pain and very cold.

Bang! Bang! Bang! Kathy is hammering on the door. "Lisa, get out of there this minute. I'm going to the movies and I have to wash my hair!"

"I'm hurrying as fast as I can," I reply.

The snow has stopped falling, and the sky is blue. A helicopter flies over the cliff. Mark waves, but the pilot doesn't see him.

Kathy yells, "Mum says you have to come out right now."

"I can't!" I say.

"You have to! You've been in there for ages."

The helicopter returns because the pilot wants to have one last look. Mark is too weak to wave, but the pilot sees his red jacket on the white snow. The helicopter lands on the top of the cliff, and someone goes down with a rope and a stretcher. Awesome! Mark is alive! He's going to be OK!

I tuck the book under my sweatshirt and unlock the door.

"All yours," I say to Kathy.

She glares at me. "You didn't flush!" Then she yells, "Mum! Lisa didn't . . ."

"I didn't need to," I tell her quickly. "I didn't go."

Kathy's eyes grow as big as doughnuts. She forgets her shower and the movies and goes running into the kitchen, yelling "Mum! Mu-u-um!"

I think I'll run down to the library.

Pavlova Queen

Rose Hudson

Our mum can't bake. She's not bad at roast dinners, school lunches, scrambled eggs, and chips, but when it comes to baking cakes, she's hopeless.

Dad bakes all the cakes in our house. His banana cakes are bliss!

One day during the school holidays, when Dad was at work, we told Mum it was time she learned to bake cakes.

"It's as easy as boiling eggs," we told her.

"You all know what happened the last time *I* boiled eggs," Mum said.

We should have remembered. The telephone rang, and Mum forgot the eggs boiling on the stove. They boiled dry, exploded, and ended up stuck to the ceiling.

"Come on, Mum, give it a go," we begged.

"Make a pav, Mum. Dad doesn't like pav. He says pavs aren't real cakes."

"Yeah, that's right. You could be the Pavlova Queen of Titahi Bay if you tried. No one around here makes pavs any more. Come on, Mum. It's my birthday tomorrow. Make me a pav for my birthday, *please*, Mum!"

"Baking's just like a science experiment, Mum. You put a bit of this and a bit of that together, give it a stir, and then wait and see if the mixture changes when it's heated up in the oven."

Mum started to look interested. She likes science. She teaches it at school.

"Well," she said slowly. "Let's read the experiment—er —recipe together and see if this pav is possible."

The picture of the pav in the recipe book looked great —big and fluffy with lots of strawberries and cream.

"You can't go wrong, Mum. You just have to beat the eggs and mix in a . . ."

"I know, I know," Mum interrupted. "A bit of this and a bit of that. OK, I'll give it a go. Dad may be the King of Banana Cakes, but I'm going to be the Queen of Pavs! Let's get started."

We carefully separated the yolks and the whites of the eggs and beat the whites till our arms ached. All four of us had a go. We beat and beat and beat the whites till they stood up like little mountains in the mixing bowl.

Then we folded in the sugar and piled the white fluffy mixture onto the oven tray, and we stood back to admire our effort.

"Looks just like the picture in the book," Mum said proudly as we licked the mixing bowl clean.

What happened next kept us glued to the oven window. Instead of rising, Mum's pav began to melt, and as it melted, it spread across the oven tray until it reached the edge. Then it dripped slowly down the sides of the oven till the drips hit the bottom element.

"Get back!" yelled Mum. She turned off the oven and opened the door. There was a sizzle, then a crackle of flame. Suddenly, the whole oven was on fire. Mum grabbed the fire extinguisher and blasted the flames. When the smoke cleared, there was the pav, black, with a dusting of white powder.

Mum was shaking her head. "And me a science teacher! I should have known you never open a burning oven. You've got fuel and heat; as soon as you add air, whoosh! it explodes."

"But what went wrong, Mum?"

"Just one of those things," she said. "Like science— you think you know what the result should be—then BANG! and things change. That's how scientists like Marie Curie and Lord Rutherford made new discoveries."

"What did you discover, Mum?" we asked.

"That you never open a burning oven, that's what! Let's leave the cakes to Dad—I'll stick to real science!"

Trapped by an Octopus

Janet Slater Bottin

There were seven kids in our family. Mum really had to stretch the money to make sure we all got enough to eat. Our meals were pretty ordinary apart from the original mixtures Mum created from recycled leftovers. Some of those were very interesting indeed! And we always had to eat up everything on our plates.

About the only time we got special treats was on birthdays and at Christmas. So party invitations were always a big deal.

"I'll make you something *different* to wear," said Mum when I told her about the fancy dress party. My heart sank. I imagined the fabulous costumes my friends' parents would hire for them, and I watched with dread as Mum started ripping an old sheet into strips.

"Oh well," I thought, "at least there'll be lots of *real* food!" My mouth watered as I thought about it—

chippies, sausage rolls, ice cream, CHOCOLATE . . .!

"SURPRISE!" said Mum.

I *was* surprised! Mum hadn't done too badly with the old sheet, after all. I giggled as I wriggled into it.

"I've stuffed all the tentacles, but I've only filled the two for your arms halfway," said Mum.

I shoved my hands into the tentacles. I could feel the stuffing halfway down—more scraps of old sheet! The other six tentacles dangled, three from the front and three from the back.

Time to go! My stomach gurgled in anticipation. I slipped into my octopus costume and slid my arms down as far as they'd go.

Mum zipped me in. My brother had made me a paper bag mask of an octopus head.

I was fully disguised.

Dancing at the fancy dress party was fun. As I spun round, the tentacles all swung out. I giggled as they thwacked the boys.

"Who *is* that octopus?" everyone asked.

At last it was suppertime. I swung across to the loaded tables. What a spread! Where should I start? Chippies?

Yeah, chicken-flavoured chippies. Then the savouries. Then the chocolate cake!

I reached out towards the chippie bowl. Suddenly, I found that I had a major problem! My hands were stuck halfway down the tentacles. I couldn't use them! No way could I take off my costume—I only had my underwear on underneath!

All I could do was stand there drooling, watching all that beautiful food slowly disappear before my ravenous eyes—trapped by an octopus!

I'll never forget it!

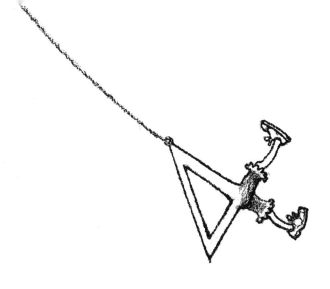

Witches Britches

Karen Sidney

Harata and her mother went shopping in town to buy Harata some new clothes. Harata's mother chose a red-striped dress for her to wear when the weather got colder.

Harata wandered up and down the shop aisles looking at the different clothes. Shirts, trousers, singlets. Then something caught her eye. It was made from red stretchy material and had white lace on the end of the legs. She held it up against her. It was a pair of underpants with long legs. Harata thought they were "Choice!" She wanted them.

Her mother came looking for her. "What have you got there?"

"Some neat pants. Can you get them for me . . . pleeease?" She looked hopefully at her mother.

"I suppose so," her mother sighed. "At least they'll be nice and warm, and you can wear them with this new dress."

The lady at the counter wrapped up the new clothes and told Harata the underpants were called "Witches Britches".

Harata was very proud of her witches britches, and wanted to wear them everywhere. Every day she put them on under her clothes. When she wore dresses and played on the jungle gym, she'd make an extra effort to jump high into the air so everyone could see the long red legs with the white lace on the end.

Sometimes at night, after her mother had made her change into her nightie, she'd climb out of bed and put the witches britches back on and sleep in them.

She tried to wear them every day, but her mother always checked and said, "No Harata, you are only allowed to wear them for one day at a time and then put them out to wash."

She looked forward to when they came in from the line all fresh and clean and she could wear them again.

One day, her family got a call from home to say their uncle had died and they got ready to go to the tangi. It was a long way and this time, instead of driving, her father said they would fly. Harata was really excited. She hadn't been on a plane before. Her mother got out the new red stripy dress and the witches britches to wear on the plane. Harata was only a little scared when the plane first took off, but she was soon feeling better and looked out the window at the land as it passed underneath. The air hostess let her take around the lolly tray. The ride was fun.

At the tangi, Harata and her cousins found lots to do around the marae. It was hotter here than in Auckland, so

Harata wore her shorts with her witches britches under them. They looked funny sticking out of the bottom of the shorts and her cousins laughed.

"Save them till when we go home on the plane—you can wear them then," her mother said.

After the tangihanga, and when everyone came back from the urupa, there was a big hakari. There was a separate table for the kids full of fizzy drinks—raspberry and orangeade — chips, lollies, trifle and jelly, riwai, meat, kumara and puha.

"Don't eat too much kai," Harata's parents warned.

"We have to catch the plane after the hakari."

Harata nodded okay then she looked at her cousins all eating and at the table again and her eyes got bigger and bigger. She stuffed herself with all the different food and drink.

A bit later, her parents came to the table to collect her to catch the plane. They said goodbye to the aunties, uncles and cousins and went to the airport.

The air hostess smiled at Harata as they boarded the plane. She sat next to the window, beside her mother, and her father sat across the aisle.

The plane started to bump around as they went through some clouds on the way to Auckland. Harata's mother said not to be scared, but she wasn't feeling scared. Instead, she was feeling sick from the bumpy ride. Her stomach hurt.

Her mother looked at her with a worried frown, "Are you feeling okay, Harata—are you feeling woozy?"

Harata opened her mouth to tell her mother she felt sick and suddenly up came the fizzy drink—

orangeade and raspberry—up came the trifle and the jelly and everything else she'd eaten—all over her stripy red dress. Oh no, what a mess! She was wearing the hakari!

"Well, you can't wear this now," said Harata's mother as she and the air hostess cleaned up. The air hostess's smile was looking a bit crooked.

The plane was just about to land at Auckland Airport.

"What will I wear?" asked Harata suddenly.

"You should have thought of that before," said Harata's mother. "I told you not to eat too much. You'll just have to wear your singlet and witches britches."

Oh no! Harata liked her witches britches, but not enough to wear them through the busy airport. How embarrassing!

They got off the plane and Harata held her mother's hand and dragged behind a little. "Come on," her mother said, pulling her along. "No one will notice." But they did! People stopped and looked. All the kids Harata's age stared and laughed. Harata stared back and pretended she always wore her witches britches like this. But it didn't work, she still felt really embarrassed and it was a very long walk to the car.

Harata didn't wear her witches britches much after that. She hid them in the back of a drawer and told her mother she couldn't find them. She just wore ordinary underpants, and she didn't jump off the jungle gym to show them off, either.

Silent Reading

David Hill

What do I do on Saturdays? I clear out the library where my mum works.

I don't clear out books or newspapers—I clear out little kids.

Heaps of little kids come to the library on Saturdays. Most of them are OK. But some shouldn't be in a library, they should be in the zoo.

A couple of Saturdays ago, one little girl kept taking books off the shelves and pushing them down the Returns slot.

"Don't do that, please," I told her. The girl kept pushing books down the slot. "Don't do that," I said again. She went and grabbed more books.

So I hid on the other side of the Returns slot. When the girl started pushing the books down, I reached up through the slot and grabbed her hand. "S-s-s-s-s," I hissed.

21

CRASH! She dropped all the books. ZOOM! She tore out of the library. "One annoying kid gone," I thought.

That same Saturday, two boys were having races around the library. They kept knocking books off shelves and banging into people.

I asked them twice to stop, but they just laughed. So I hid inside the big cupboard where the library vacuum cleaner is kept. When the boys ran past, I pushed the vacuum cleaner hose through the door so that it looked like a snake coming out.

"I am the library ghost," I groaned. *"Who-o-o-o."*

"A-a-a-a-argh!" the boys gasped. They galloped out of the library. "Three annoying kids gone," I thought.

Then last Saturday, two little kids started chucking round the big cushions in the reading corner. They threw the cushions across the floor, nearly tripping people up. "Stop that, please," I said. They kept throwing. "Don't!" I said. They threw harder.

So I got a long piece of string from Mum's desk. I tied it to a corner of one cushion, and I put the cushion near some shelves. I hid on the other side, holding the string.

The two kids came racing down the row of shelves. They saw my cushion and grabbed for it.

I pulled the string. The cushion slid across the carpet and disappeared under the shelf. It must have looked as if it was moving by itself.

"Come on, cushions," I called in a moaning voice. "Let's go and find those nasty little cushion-chuckers."

GLOP! Two mouths fell open. ZIP! Two people hurtled for the door. "Five annoying little kids gone," I thought.

A bit later last Saturday, two little girls were sticking their hands into the library's goldfish tank, trying to catch the goldfish.

"Leave the fish alone," I said. They laughed at me. "Those fish bite!" I said. They laughed even louder, but they went off to jump on the beanbags.

Then I remembered something. In the library's toy-box was a massive plastic doll with one arm missing. I grabbed it and twisted the other arm off. It was nearly as big as a real arm. I pulled one of my own arms out of my sweatshirt and stuck the doll's arm up my sleeve. Then I waited by the goldfish tank.

When the two girls appeared again, I pretended to reach into the tank. Then I let the doll's arm splash into the water. "My arm!" I went. "The fish bit my arm off!"

The girls stared at the arm lying in the tank. "OHHHH!" they wailed. VAROOM! They sprinted off. "*Seven* annoying little kids gone," I thought.

So that's what I do on Saturdays—I clear out kids from the library.

But, last night, I heard Mum telling Uncle Joel how hardly any little kids come to the library any more. She said some kids have told their mothers there are hand-grabbing hissers, groaning ghosts, cushion-monsters and dangerous sharks in the library.

"Something's going on," said Mum. She gave me a look.

I think . . . I think that this Saturday I'll clear out my room instead.

The Super-Trolley

Cynthia Todd Maguire

Gary and I have got this *excellent* idea for our trolley. We're going to make it bigger and heavier and faster. We've challenged Mark and Greg to a race this afternoon, and this morning we've been all the way down to the tip on our bikes. Half an hour there and back. Scratching around with the seagulls and pukeko. We got what we were looking for though. A pair of really *big* pram wheels.

We're getting stuck into the trolley when Mum comes along, worrying about my using Dad's good wood. Does Mum really think I'm stupid or something? I know better than that . . . now. I got my TV time docked for a month after *that* episode.

"No way, Mum. I'm only using the old stuff that's stacked behind the water tank."

"Good." Now we can get going again.

Next thing, Jonny's out here, too. He's my three-year-old brother.

"He only wants to watch you work," Mum says when she sees me make a face. "Little ones learn by looking. You were the same when you were that age. Where'd you get the nails?" Mum sounds suspicious.

"They're the bent ones Mr Lake gave me when he was building his house. Remember? I bang them straight and use them again."

Mum nods, then comes out with: "Don't drop any nails in the grass." Jonny picks a nail up.

"What's that?" says Mum triumphantly. Thanks a lot, Jonny!

"If a nail wrecks the lawnmower or gives us a puncture, you'll have to pay for the repairs," she warns.

"Yes, Mum." Please, go away!

"Where're you going to have your race today?"

"Mozzie Hill."

"Mozzie Hill?" Mum explodes. That's Mum's name for the track, because the mosquitoes lie in wait for her where the seat is, halfway up. The track's steep and curvy. She's out of breath by the time she gets there . . . and collapses. That's when the mozzies strike their sitting target. "Can't you pick a gentler slope?"

"Oh, *Mum*, there'd be no *fun*!"

We widen and lengthen the trolley. Bigger, heavier, faster. The more wood we nail on, the more Mum worries.

"If you make it too heavy, the trolley'll break up, and you'll hurt yourselves."

"Don't worry, Mum. Trust me!"

Jonny gets too close to a hammer striking wood. This gives me a good reason to tell Mum it's too dangerous for him here. She agrees and takes him away. At last! Now Gary and I can get on with the job.

We get the old wheels off and the new bigger ones on and put a new beer crate on, for a seat.

At exactly the same moment, Gary and I notice the concrete blocks Dad stores under the verandah. Dad leaves two there, to use as chocks when the car's parked on our steep drive. Gary and I grin at each other. Hold our thumbs up. Choice. Just what we need to make ours a super-trolley. Except we don't want to let Mum see us tie a block on. We wait till we're out the gate, then fetch the block from behind the pohutukawa tree. Gary had run down and hidden it there, while I distracted Mum and Jonny. Well, you can't muck about when you want to win. Now we're sure of success. We'll show Mark and Greg.

We get in position at the top of Mozzie Hill.

Gary and I are shocked to see Mark and Greg have gone one step bigger—*bike* wheels! No worries. We're built for speed. We have the skill . . . and the technology!

The two trolleys take off in a burst after the starting push, come together and miss each other by a dog's whisker. Then Mark swerves to avoid a tree, heads straight down instead of around the curve, and skids into the ditch at the side of the track. Greg runs down and helps him out.

I take the curve well and zoom around and down just as Mark gets his trolley back on the track. I bounce off him so he lurches sideways and slithers along a clay bank. Nice one! I bump ahead, crash . . . against a stone. Ouch!

Gary catches up with me and helps right the trolley. We check it out for damage. No problem. Except now Mark's streaking past us screaming and yahooing.

We can make up lost time only if Mark comes to grief somewhere. We're in luck. He strikes a hole, I clip his trolley as I pass. Go round a bend. Something catches my eye behind me, it's Mark, tearing straight down the slope . . . he's missed the track again. My trolley skids on a patch of pine needles and swerves towards Mark's. The steepest part of the track. The concrete block is pulling me forwards. We've outdone ourselves, I realise. Gary and me. We're too heavy. Too heavy. Those words sound familiar. Somebody had warned us today. Who? Too heavy. I up-end. Mark crunches into me. Two bodies and trolleys fly in different directions. Mark is the lucky one. He sails into the sand at the bottom of the track. Gary finds me sprawled out in the middle of a toitoi bush, toitoi feathers "raining' on me. Ouch again! Mark and Greg's trolley has a wheel off, the seat's come adrift, and their mother's cushion has disappeared! Our trolley, our super-trolley is broken completely in half, shattered and splintered. We're able to rescue a bit of it, a very small bit.

It's humiliating . . . coming up the road, dangling two front wheels on a rope.

Mum's watching out the kitchen window when we get home. I bet she feels really sorry for us, having no trolley now.

"No worries, Mum," I call up to her as we trudge up the drive. "Gary and I have got this excellent idea for a go-kart!"

Uncle Trev and the Light Bulb

Jack Lasenby

"What are you doing?" my mother said. "That light bulb's dead. Anyway, I thought I've told you not to play around with electricity."

"I'm just putting it in so there's something in the socket," I told her.

"Well, you needn't bother. I want you to go down to the shop for me, and you can get yourself a new bulb while you're about it."

"Yes," I said, "but you've got to keep something in the socket."

"Why?"

"Because Uncle Trev said so."

"Said what?" asked my mother. "Come on, what's that uncle of yours been telling you now?"

"He said if you don't have a bulb in the socket and you turn on the switch, all the electricity inside the wire runs out into your room."

"It what?"

I explained it again. "I've never heard the like of it!" my mother said. "There's more daft ideas inside that man's head than there are days in a year! Where on earth did he get that one from?"

"It's true," I said. "It's got to be. Otherwise, why do you have a switch?"

"The electricity doesn't work unless there's something in the socket," Mum said. "It's something to do with it being a circuit, the man from the power board told me. It goes round and round like water, he said. You have a switch to stop it from being wasted."

"Yes," I said, "Uncle Trev says it's like water too. But he said, 'What happens to the electricity in the wire when you take the bulb out and leave the switch on?' He reckons it's like leaving a tap running. It's got to go somewhere, he says."

"Oh, I don't know! Here, run down to the shop. Get the bread and paper, and get yourself a light bulb and put it in. Perhaps that will stop you worrying."

"What size?"

"A forty's all you need. In any case, you shouldn't be reading in bed till all hours, straining your eyes."

"Uncle Trev says his old pressure lamp's better for reading by," I said. "He reckons kerosene lamps are better than anything, because they give a softer light. He says we don't know much about electricity yet."

"You could have been down to the shop and back a dozen times while you've been standing there talking," Mum said. "Why your uncle thinks he knows anything about electricity, I don't know. Isn't he the only farmer out on his road who won't have the electricity put on, and isn't that only because he's scared of it? Well," she said, "are you going to get that light bulb or not?"

I ran to the shop. Uncle Trev was just coming out the door. "I'll give you a lift home, if you hurry," he said. "Take your time." I never quite knew exactly what Uncle Trev meant.

When I came out with the light bulb, he looked at it and said, "I hope you left the dead bulb in the socket."

"Yes, but Mum said it's nonsense about the electricity running out of the socket and leaking into the room."

"Well," he said, "she's a knowledgeable woman, your mother," and he drove round to our place.

"The power board's talking of putting up poles along our road," he said as we pulled up. "But they want everyone to say they'll have the power on before they'll do it. They'll never get me to have electricity running all through my house, leaking out of the light sockets, just waiting for a chance to give me a shock," he said as we went along the side of the house.

"What's all this nonsense I hear about electricity running out of the light sockets?" Mum demanded the moment we got in the door.

"Nonsense, is it?" Uncle Trev said. "I'll tell you what— when we came in that back door, I could tell there was a switch left on somewhere in your house by the way the hair stood up on the back on my neck. There's no surer sign."

I ran my hand up the back of my neck. "My hair's standing on end too," I said.

"That's because you've just had it cut," said my mother. "Now you go at once and put that bulb in your light and make sure you pull the switch off first."

I looked at the light cord hanging from beside the switch in the middle of the room and couldn't remember whether I'd pulled it on or off. Maybe Uncle Trev was right, maybe the room was full of electricity that had leaked out and was running around waiting to electrify me when I put in the bulb. I went back to the kitchen.

"Well," Mum said. "Is that better?"

I said nothing. "Well?" she said again. She saw the light bulb in my hand. "What's the matter now? Why haven't you put it in? You can reach it if you stand on a chair."

"I can't remember whether I pulled the cord on or off," I said.

"Oh, I never heard the like of it!" Mum snatched the bulb out of my hand. "I'll do it myself, then I'll be sure it's done. It's like talking to yourself, expecting anyone to do anything round this place!"

As she stormed out to my room, Uncle Trev jumped up and turned off something on the switchboard by the back door. He'd just sat down again when Mum came back.

"That's funny," she said. "That bulb you bought must be dead. You'll have to take it back and change it. I can't get it to go."

I went out with her. I pulled on the light cord, and the bulb went on. "It's all right," I said, and pulled it off again. I pulled it, and the light went again. "Probably I've got more electricity in my body through sleeping in here without a

31

bulb in the socket. The switch must have been on, so it was all leaking into the room like Uncle Trev said."

"Here!" Mum pulled the cord. The bulb was dead. "What's going on? Here, you have a go." I pulled the cord, and the light came on. I pulled it off, and Mum had another go. Again, the bulb was dead.

We went out to the kitchen. Uncle Trev was standing up from the table, as if coming out to help us.

"Don't you go touching it," Mum told him. "It's bound to go wrong if you lay a finger on it." She tried the kitchen light and it went on. "There!" she said and marched out to my room. Uncle Trev leapt and turned off something on the switchboard.

Mum almost caught him that time. She swept back in but thought he was coming to help again. "I don't know what it can be," she said. "You'd better have another go."

When I told her it worked, she said, "Oh well, it's your light after all, so it doesn't matter much whether I can get it to go or not, I suppose."

"I was reading somewhere," said Uncle Trev, "in the *Herald* or maybe the *Weekly News*, that some people have more electricity in their bodies than others. I'm sure there's still a lot for us to understand about it." He looked at me and rubbed the side of his nose. I didn't dare rub mine back at him, because Mum was watching us.

"Anyway," she said, "it's a blessing, the power, when it works."

"I'm sure it must be," said my uncle.

Circus Routine

Diana Noonan

"I saw it!" shouted Jay Stokes. "I saw the circus poster in the window of Whittler's dairy." She did a cartwheel on the netball court and came running into the classroom. "Who's going?"

There was a buzz of excitement. Stevie and I looked at each other.

"Don't you like the circus?" asked Mr Kapa, handing out our maths books. We didn't say a word. We loved the circus, and we knew we'd get to go. It was what Dad expected us to do to earn our ticket money that was the problem. Just the thought made my cheeks burn with embarrassment. If only we didn't live beside the showgrounds. If only Dad didn't grow tomatoes.

It wasn't until the following Thursday that the circus trucks rolled into town. Mr Kapa let us out of class to watch them pass. I held my breath, hoping like anything that somehow, the elephants wouldn't arrive this year. There was always a minuscule chance that some terrible pachyderm plague had swept the country, or that maybe the elephants had misbehaved and got sent to a zoo.

"There go the elephants!" shrieked Jay.

I wished I could disappear.

The next afternoon when we got home from school, Dad had the wheelbarrow parked in the drive. He came out of the glasshouse grinning and rubbing his hands together like he'd just discovered gold.

"Right you two! Overalls on. I've checked everything out with the manager. They're expecting you."

"Couldn't we go later?" asked Stevie.

"Like after dark," I mumbled.

"Now!" said Dad firmly, and when he looked over at the compost heap, his eyes were sparkling.

I pushed the barrow out our back gate and into the showgrounds. The long summer grass came right up to our waists, and over the seedheads we squinted into the late afternoon sun, desperately hoping we'd be able to identify anyone from school before they saw us.

"All clear, I reckon," said Stevie, when we got close to the big top. "Let's go."

Ahead of us, we saw the field where the elephants had been grazing. It was dotted with their droppings.

"If anyone from school sees us picking up this stuff, we're dead," I said. I could just hear the jokes that would fly round class. It was too awful to think about.

"You load and I'll keep watch," I said, taking charge. "I'll whistle if I see anyone we know. If you hear me, drop

34

the shovel, and act like we've come over to suss out the animals."

"In our overalls?"

I shrugged. "Just do it."

By the fourth trip, we were into a pretty cool routine. Even so, twice we had to dive for cover in the long grass to avoid being spotted.

At home, the compost heap grew higher and higher. Dad was beside himself with delight. He kept asking if we'd got every last shovelful. "After all," he said, "it's not every day that a circus parks next door to your glass-house!"

It was a major relief when, after four days of our collecting that stuff, he finally produced the tickets for the Saturday night circus performance. There were three.

"I'm coming with you," he said. "I haven't been to a circus for years."

Dad had got the best seats; right down the front where you can see everything because there are no heads in the way. The show was better than ever, and when they dimmed the lights for the trapeze artists and shone sparkling stars on the roof of the big top, I felt like I was floating through the universe.

It was the elephants' performance in the next act that reminded me we were definitely back on earth. There they were, the four of them, linked trunk to tail, lumbering round the ring in time to the brass band music. It was such an amazing sight that I bet no one in the whole audience noticed what happened next; no one, that is, except Stevie and Dad and I.

One minute the sawdust in the ring was clean as a whistle, and the next, this cute clown came hurrying out with a bucket and spade to clean up after an elephant.

Beside me, Dad shuffled in his seat. He wasn't looking at the elephants any more. He was watching the bucket disappear through a slit in the tent.

"Where's he taking it?" he asked, but I refused to answer.

It was only later, when the show was over and we were outside talking to some friends from school, that I realised Dad was still thinking about it.

"I'll have those," he said, snatching our giant popcorn containers from our hands.

"Why?" I asked.

"Because I didn't bring the wheelbarrow," he hissed, heading for a side door in the tent.

"Where's your dad going?" asked Jay Stokes.

I stood there with my mouth wide open. I didn't know what to say. It was Stevie who came to the rescue.

"Ah, he knows the manager. He's probably gone to congratulate him on the show."

I felt my face turn scarlet. "He could be talking for hours," I said, quickly nudging Stevie into the crowd flowing out from the tent. "There's no point waiting for him."

Around us, people closed in on all sides. I was feeling safer by the minute.

"Wow!" said Jay, tagging along. "So your father's talking to the manager!" She sounded impressed. "He sure knows the big guys."

Stevie mumbled something in my ear and pushed me further into the crowd. I tried to keep a straight face.

"Big guys?" I said to Jay. I was starting to grin. "Oh sure. In fact, not many people round town know just how big some of Dad's circus friends actually are!"

Roimata and the Forest of Tane

Miriam Smith

Roimata and Granny lived in an old, old house.

Granny was even older than the house. Roimata was sure that Granny was at least one hundred years old.

In front of their house grew a tall tawa tree.

"Why don't you cut it down?" Granny's sons would ask. "It shades the house, and the leaves mess up the lawn."

But Granny would just smile, and they gave up asking.

Roimata and Granny had their favourite thinking places. Roimata's favourite place was a swing on the tawa tree. Granny's was her rocking chair on the verandah.

Roimata liked the shadowy patterns made by the sun on the tree. And she liked the way the dry leaves crackled under her feet. It was like walking on cornflakes.

The tawa bark was dark and smooth, with little bits of green lichen growing on it.

If Roimata looked closely, she could see it was covered

with lines like the lines on Granny's face.

It was autumn. The tawa berries were ripe. They hung from the tree like dark purple plums.

Granny sat rocking in her chair.

Roimata leaned back on her swing, looking upwards at the leaves, the sky, and the berries.

"Did you ever eat these berries, Granny?" Roimata asked.

"When I was a little girl," said Granny, "my mother used to soak the berries and dry them. They were good cooked in a hangi. They tasted like mashed potatoes. In those days, the forest was so important to us. Do you know, my mother used this tree to make medicine for cuts and tummy aches and colds."

"Did you have a swing like this one?"

"No," said Granny, "but I was a good climber. I used to hide there in the branches where nobody could see me. Long ago, Roimata, this tree was on the edge of a forest. Now all the other trees are gone."

"Is that why you call it the forest of Tane?" asked Roimata.

Granny smiled and nodded. "Yes, because now it's the only tree left in the forest of Tane, as I knew it.

"In those days the pigeons used to come to eat the berries. They had great feasts. They ate so many that they grew fat and heavy.

"Tuis would come too, and nest on the branches. Sometimes they coughed and clucked. But other times they made beautiful tui music.

"On still nights, a morepork would visit the tree. I used to hear it calling to its mate—morepork, morepork . . ."

"Morepork, morepork," called Roimata to the branches.

Granny went on, "My father cut down part of the forest when he built this house. He left the tawa tree there for the birds. But later he sold the land, and soon all the forest was cut down.

"When people came, they built houses and roads and made the town. Because the trees were gone, there was nowhere for the birds to live, and no food for them to eat.

"This old tree stood here in the garden all the time I was growing up. Then I got married, and your mother was born, and then your two uncles. When they were all little, they had a swing on the tree—just like yours.

"The house was very quiet after they grew up and left home. And then two years ago your grandfather died. I was very lonely—that's when you came to live with me."

"I think," said Roimata, "that this tree must have been growing forever."

She shut her eyes and imagined she was in the forest of Tane. She listened for the beautiful music, but all she could hear was the sound of traffic.

That night, there was a fierce storm.

Roimata didn't like storms, so she got into Granny's bed. Each time the lightning flashed, it lit up the room. Roimata and Granny waited for the thunder to follow. The wind howled around the house. There were strange groaning sounds, and then—a loud CRASH!

The tawa tree had blown down.

The next day Roimata and Granny sat on the verandah and looked sadly at their tree.

Granny's sons came with a chainsaw and cut up the tree.

"We always thought it was dangerous," they said.

They made a tidy heap of the small branches and leaves and took the rest away for firewood.

Autumn turned to winter.

Roimata and Granny seldom went outside.

Granny dozed in her chair by the fire. Sometimes she talked of the old days in the forest of Tane. Roimata thought of the tawa tree with sunlight on its branches.

When spring came, Granny's sons brought a truck. They cleared away the heap of leaves and branches which had been on the garden all winter.

"Come on Roimata," they said, "you can tidy up the last of the leaves."

Roimata slowly raked the leaves into a pile—it was then she saw them!

In the shelter of the leaves and branches of the old tree, three little trees had begun to grow. Their leaves were long and thin like those of the tawa.

"Granny! Granny!" called Roimata, "the forest of Tane is growing again."

That day, Granny brought her chair out into the warm spring sunshine. As she sat and rocked, Roimata talked of how she would care for the young trees.

"Summer will soon be here," she said. "I'll need to water them every day. Some day, when I'm a granny like you, I think I'll put a swing on one of those trees—for my grandchildren."

Granny smiled—and nodded.

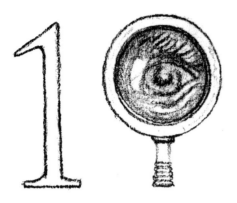

The Case of the Phantom Tagger

Margaret Schroder

Can you find out "whodunnit" before Inspector Edwards?

Inspector Edwards was on holiday and pleased to be away from the stresses of crime solving. He was relaxing on a sun-lounger by the hotel swimming pool with a glass of chilled orange juice in his hand when a commotion at the far end of the pool caught his eye. Three protesting boys were being marched along by an angry-looking hotel porter. Normally, Inspector Edwards would have ignored the whole scene. He was on holiday. Someone else could solve the problem. Unfortunately, one of the protesting boys was his elder son.

Abandoning his orange juice, the inspector walked over to the porter.

"Good afternoon," he said politely. He signalled to his son to keep quiet. "I'm Inspector Edwards, chief crime-solver with Central Police. What seems to be the trouble here?"

The hotel porter paused briefly. "A police inspector, eh? Maybe you can help. I'm taking these vandals to the manager's office. You can join me if you like."

When they were all assembled in the manager's office, Inspector Edwards reached into the pocket of his floral shirt and took out his trusty notebook and pen. The porter began his story.

"I checked the children's games room at 1.30 p.m.," he said. "These three boys were the only ones there. Everything seemed in order, so I left. Ten minutes later I passed by again, and when I put my head round the door just to check everything was still OK, I found that some vandal had scribbled a tag right along the side of the pool table. This marker pen was stuffed into one of the pool-table pockets." He held out the evidence. "I asked the boys if anyone else had come into the games room while they'd been there, and they said no. When I showed them the tagging, they all denied doing it. One of them is lying, but how can we find out which one?"

"Do you mind if I check out their stories?" asked the inspector.

"Go ahead," said the manager.

Inspector Edwards tapped his pen on his notebook and looked at the boys. "I want each of you to tell me your name and what you were doing just before the porter came into the games room for the second time," he said. "We'll start with you."

"I'm Mark," said the first boy. "I was playing one of the spacies. I had my back to the pool table, and the

43

machine was making a lot of noise, so I didn't hear or see anything."

Inspector Edwards made a short note and pointed to his son. "You're next."

"I'm Peter. I was playing darts at the far end of the room. I had my back to the pool table, too. I was concentrating so hard on my game that I didn't see anything either."

"That just leaves you," said the inspector, pointing to the third boy. "What's your story?"

"I'm Luke. I was in the library corner reading *Surfing in Switzerland*. Surfing and body-boarding are my hobbies—ask anyone. I had my back to the pool table as well. I didn't see anything."

The inspector made a final note.

"If none of these boys will own up," said the manager, "they'll *all* have to pay for the damage."

"That won't be necessary," replied Inspector Edwards. "I know which one isn't telling the truth."

DO YOU? The answer is on page 126.

Mayday!

Christine Ashton

Ben waited until he was sure Mum and Nick were asleep. Then he bundled up his sleeping bag and crept downstairs. It was hard to move quietly through a strange place in the dark. He stubbed his toe on the edge of the hearth and gasped. The front door squeaked when he opened it, and he froze, listening carefully in case he had woken anyone.

Outside, he switched on his torch and made his way down the long drive to where the boat was parked at the back of the section. They'd had a great weekend sailing *Kestrel* on Lake Te Anau, but now she was on her trailer behind their friend's house.

With the rigging wires looping everywhere, climbing aboard was awkward. The boom now occupied the berth Ben had slept in. He found another and unrolled his sleeping bag onto it. Although he missed the sound of water lapping against the hull, it felt good to be on board *Kestrel* again. He wriggled into the sleeping bag, closed his eyes, and drifted into sleep.

It was still dark when Ben was woken by the movement of the boat. He reached for his torch, felt sail bags instead, and remembered that the holiday was over. Nick couldn't be hitching the boat trailer to the car. They were leaving *Kestrel* here till they came again at Christmas. Outside, an engine rumbled softly. Footsteps crunched on the gravel. Then Ben realised that the vehicle he could hear didn't sound like Nick's car. He looked back at the crib. There were no lights on.

Outside, an unfamiliar voice hissed, "Hurry up! Get that thing on." For a moment, Ben thought he heard someone climb onto the boat. He lay low in the bunk, his heart hammering. Someone swore, doors closed softly, and suddenly the trailer, with Ben and the boat on it, was moving. As it turned out of the drive, Ben peeked out and saw that it was being towed by a ute. Someone was stealing *Kestrel*!

The trailer was now moving too fast for him to jump. There had to be something he could do. His mind was a whirr. The radio? A mayday call? *Kestrel* wasn't sinking, but she was certainly in trouble. Ben turned on the set. His fingers fumbled nervously with the switches. Nick had said channel sixteen was the emergency channel.

The radio crackled into life. "Mayday, mayday, mayday!" Ben called. He waited. No answer. "Mayday, mayday. *Kestrel* calling. Can anyone hear me?" The boat was slowing down. What if whoever was stealing her had a radio in the ute and could hear him? He peered out, but the vehicle was only slowing to take a corner.

Ben jumped with fright as a voice spoke from the cabin. "Mayday, *Kestrel*. This is the *Ellie Sue*. Received your mayday. What is your position?"

"I don't know," stammered Ben into the microphone. "I mean, the boat is on a trailer. It's being towed."

"Sonny, if you're playing with the radio, you'd better get off it smartly. This is the emergency channel."

"I'm not playing. This is a real emergency. Someone is stealing our boat—and I'm inside it."

"Oh! Right." The voice sounded surprised. "Do you know your position, *Kestrel*? I mean, do you know where you are?"

"We were parked in Te Anau. We're out of the town now, but we haven't been driving long."

"OK. That narrows it down. I'm leaving you temporarily to contact the police."

A new voice came on the radio. "*Kestrel. Kestrel*. The *Aquito* here. Te Anau's my home area. Can you see out?"

Ben peered out the cabin window. "Sort of. It's pretty dark."

"Watch out for anything that will tell us which road you're on."

Ben had no idea who he was talking to, or where they were. It didn't matter as long as they could help. He pressed his nose against the cabin window. There were just fields for what seemed like ages.

"You OK there?" The voice from the *Ellie Sue* was speaking to him again. "What does your boat look like?"

"It's a trailer yacht. It's got a red hull and white deck."

"What sort of vehicle is towing it?"

47

"A ute—a white one. Hold on! We're slowing down. I can see water out the window."

"A lake?"

"I think so. We've just gone round a really tight corner."

The voice from the *Aquito* cut in. "That'll be Manapouri."

There were very few houses and then fields again. Ben didn't have to wait long before the trailer slowed again.

"We've just turned right," he spoke into the microphone. "There was a signpost, but it was too dark to read it."

"*Aquito* here. Don't worry. They must be heading down the Blackmount road. It's the only one on the right. *Ellie Sue* is relaying the information to the police. They're not far behind you. How are you feeling?"

"I'm OK," said Ben. He wasn't going to tell anyone how scared he really was. "Where are you?"

"On my work boat in Milford Sound. The *Ellie Sue* is fishing in Doubtful."

They kept up a steady conversation after that. Erik told Ben all about his work on the *Aquito*. Ben told Erik about *Kestrel*; about how they'd got her cheap because she'd spent years stored away in a hay barn, covered in bird droppings. Mum and Nick and he had scrubbed her inside and out. They'd painted and varnished her until she looked like new—and now someone had the nerve to steal her! Ben liked talking. It made him feel less alone, but he wished the police would hurry.

Then, as if out of nowhere, red and blue lights lit up the inside of the cabin. A siren screamed. The trailer slowed down. The night was alive with action.

"They're here. The police are here! I have to go," Ben shouted into the radio. "Thanks for everything—over."

When it was all over and Ben was back at the crib, his mother held him tight. "I wasn't in any danger," he said. "The police made me keep down in the cabin until it was all over. I didn't even see anyone get arrested."

"But what were you doing on the boat in the first place?" asked Mum. "You could have been hurt."

"Sorry," mumbled Ben. "I just wanted to sleep one more night on *Kestrel* before we went home."

"Fair enough," said Nick, "but next time you decide to sleep on a boat, take one of us along with you—just in case you need a hand to fend off pirates!"

Green Marmalade to You

Margaret Mahy

There was once a boy called Clutha who lived with a cat and a crocodile, and they were very happy together. The strange thing was that each of them spoke a different language from the other two so that ordinary conversation was full of guesses and question marks. However, mostly they understood each other very well.

One day they all got up together, and each one of them opened his bedroom door at exactly the same time as the other two.

"Good morning," said Clutha.

"Gone mooning," said the cat.

"Green marmalade!" cried the crocodile.

(But they all meant the same thing really.)

"It's a lovely day, isn't it?" called Clutha.

"It's a lively doe, isn't it?" observed the cat.

"Ladylike Ding-Dong!" exclaimed the crocodile,

putting up its blue frilly sunshade to prove it.

(But, as you will have guessed, they all meant the same thing really.)

Now the problem was to find something they all liked for breakfast. Clutha wanted porridge, and the cat said he wanted chops (though he may have meant chips.) As for the crocodile, it couldn't choose between cheese and cherries so they decided to have something totally different.

"How about bacon and eggs?" asked Clutha. "Very tasty, bacon and eggs!"

"Break-in and exit! Very toasty!" agreed the cat.

"Broken explosions. Very twisty!" the crocodile concurred twirling its blue sunshade.

So they had broken explosions for breakfast and they enjoyed them very much. But after breakfast there is always a problem, as you know. Dirty dishes!

"We'd better do the washing up, I suppose," said Clutha.

"We'd batter down the swishing cup," nodded the cat.

"Buttered clown is wishing out," finished the croc-odile—or it sounded like that.

So they did the dishes and then they went out to play.

Now, maybe one green marmalade you'll wake up on a ladylike ding-dong and have broken explosions for breakfast too—you'll find them very twisty! But don't forget to butter the clown and swish the cup when you do the wishing out, will you?

Parent Help?

Anna Kenna

I wish, I wish, I wish I hadn't opened my big mouth and told Mum that I was lonely at school. Dumb move! That's why she decided to come with me.

I'd been feeling stink all week because I'd only just made my first friend at my new school, and suddenly she'd had to shift away to Auckland. Mum caught me crying about it. She hates it when I cry.

"My poor possum," she said as I snivelled into her sweatshirt, "this is awful. What can we do?"

That's when she came up with the terrible idea.

"Right," she said, leaping off the sofa. "I'm coming with you. Tomorrow. I'll be your best mate until you find a new friend."

I thought she was joking. I started to smile. "But, Mum, you . . ."

"No, kitten," she said, "you don't have to thank me. I *want* to do it."

Next thing, she pulled out her old tramping pack and started throwing stuff in: a pad, pencils, Dad's calculator, her knitting, and her very best thing, a pendant carved out of a whale's jawbone.

"Have we got fitness tomorrow?" she asked, grabbing her aerobics shorts. (They're highlighter-pen orange and *really* tight.)

"No!" I yelled. "I mean, no—no, we haven't."

"Well, then, I think that's about everything," said Mum, doing up the straps on her pack. "I'll pump up my bike tyres after tea. This is going to be fun!"

Next morning, I said that I had a bad headache. Mum said it was just because I was lonely at school. "Now that you've got someone to hang out with," she smiled, "you'll soon be feeling heaps better."

I prayed that a tornado would flatten our house and that we'd have to miss school to go on the TV news. No such luck. Ten minutes later, I'm riding down the hill with my mother— my mother in a bright yellow skid-lid with "Save the Whales" and "Hands off Our Rainforest" stickers all over it.

Mrs Kelly raised her eyebrows as we walked into the classroom. "Ah, Mrs Beale, I didn't have you down for parent help today."

I died. Right there, in front of Michael Connors.

"No, no, I'm not here as parent help," said Mum, heaving off her pack. "I'm here to keep Laura company. Where shall I sit?"

At first, the other kids looked shocked. Then they started to giggle.

"Stop that noise!" warned Mrs Kelly. She gave Mum the spare desk down the back.

Mum was pretty quiet during language except that she told Mrs Kelly that she'd spelt "environment" wrong. Mrs Kelly looked furious. The chalk snapped as she corrected the word. I gave Mum my fiercest frown. The kids were wetting themselves.

At morning interval, Mum got crabby about people dropping litter. "You kids have no respect for the environment," she said. She made Marcus Anderson and Lawrence Getty pick up their empty chippie bags. Then she grabbed my arm. "We've still got ten minutes," she said. "Let's go to the adventure playground."

Mostly, you have to line up for the flying fox, but when Mum arrived, kids scattered. She jumped on and swung back and forth, whooping at the top of her voice. I'm used to my mum; I've known her all my life. But some of the kids were like, "Wow! Is she for real?"

After break, we got to do some clay modelling. Mum was very loud, telling everybody what to do. Michael Connors got loud back, and Mrs Kelly sent him into the corridor to cool off. But she couldn't send a mother out, so she just glared at Mum. That was when Karla Jones came over to me.

"Mums can be real pains," she whispered, giving me some of her spare clay. She looked like she was really sorry for me. "Want to come and share my desk?"

I was so relieved when lunchtime came, except that Mum used the staffroom microwave to reheat her pasta and then had an argument with some girls who were swapping Spice Girl stickers.

"Chill out, Mum!" I hissed.

"Sorry, dear," she said. "I just happen to think that Ginger was the best."

After lunch, at news time, Nigel Lewis showed us a half-dead spider in a jar, Yang Hong said he had new Rollerblades, and Chloe Masters twiddled with her cardigan buttons and then sat down again.

Mum put up her hand and said that she had something to share. She marched up to the front of the room, and I wished that I could be kidnapped by aliens.

"Now," she said, taking out her whalebone pendant and sounding just like a teacher, "who knows what this is?"

"It's a Maori necklace," said someone down the back.

"It's an ant's tooth," joked someone else.

Everyone laughed. I put my head down on my desk as Mum began talking, but after a while I noticed that the class had gone quiet. They were actually listening. Mum told everyone heaps about whales. She even said some stuff that I hadn't heard before. When she said that some people still kill whales for food and to make lipstick and soap, everyone said that that wasn't fair. I think Karla Jones was even crying.

Mum put on a tape after that. It was of whales calling to one another under the water. I crossed my fingers that she wouldn't tell everyone the story of how she used to press the tape recorder to her tummy and play the calls to me before I was born. The tape finished just as the after-school bell went. No one moved—well, not right away.

Later, as Mum was packing up, Mrs Kelly came over and asked if she could borrow the whale tape to play to the class again.

"I thought that your talk was very interesting, Mrs Beale," she said.

Out of the corner of my eye, I saw Karla hanging around waiting for us. On the way to the gate, she told us how last summer holidays she'd helped her dad save some whales that were stuck on a beach up north.

"We stayed with them all night," she said with a faraway look in her eyes. For once, Mum didn't say anything, but I had an idea.

"Do you want to come over?" I asked. "We've just got this cool computer game. You get points for saving endangered animals."

"OK," said Karla. "I'll just check in with Mum first."

At home that night, Dad asked Mum if she'd like to go to Taupo with him next day. He said that he had some deliveries to do. Mum looked at me.

"Don't worry," I said quickly. "I'll be cool as."

"Are you sure?" she asked. "I don't mind coming to school with you again."

"Na, no sweat, Mum," I told her. "Karla's calling in for me in the morning. You go with Dad and enjoy yourself." Please!

Leila's Lunch

Jane Buxton

Leila didn't even bother to unwrap her sandwiches at lunchtime. She knew they'd be peanut butter again. She was sick of telling Mum not to give her peanut butter.

"Peanut butter sandwiches again!" she said to Sam.

"Yum," said Sam. "I love peanut butter. We never have it."

"Swap you, then," Leila said.

"Sure," said Sam happily. "You can have my tuna sandwiches." He took Leila's sandwiches and skipped away.

"What is tuna?" asked Leila, unwrapping Sam's sandwiches. She had a sniff. "Pooh! It's fish! Hey, Amber, do you like tuna sandwiches?"

"Delicious!" said Amber. "Can I have one?"

"You can have them all," Leila said, pulling a face.

"But then you'll be hungry," Amber said. "Here, you'd better have my cake."

"Ooh! Thanks, Amber," said Leila. But when she unwrapped it, she found it was carrot cake. "Boring old carrot cake," she sighed. "Mum makes that all the time."

Jeremy heard her. "Carrot cake!" he exclaimed. "That's my favourite!"

"What will you swap me for it?" Leila asked.

"I'll give you some sandwiches," said Jeremy, pulling a face. "I got them from Sam. They're so weird! You'll never guess what's in them." He held the sandwiches out to Leila. "Ook puke! Marmite and banana!"

"Marmite and banana!" cried Leila. "My favourite! Thanks, Jeremy!"

The sandwiches were delicious. Leila ate every bit of them, even the crusts.

When she got home after school, Leila said, "Mum! Guess what I had for lunch today! Marmite and banana sandwiches!"

"I thought you'd be pleased," said Mum. "I knew you were sick of peanut butter."

Leila stared at Mum. "But . . . you gave me peanut butter sandwiches. I swapped my carrot cake for the marmite and banana ones."

"No, dear," said Mum. "I didn't give you any carrot cake today."

Leila shook her head. "No! I mean Amber swapped me the cake for Sam's tuna sandwiches."

"I see . . .," said Mum, as if she didn't see at all. "And what did you give Sam?"

"My peanut butter sandwiches," said Leila. "Oh! But they weren't . . .?"

"No," Mum said. "They weren't peanut butter sand-wiches—they were . . ."

"Marmite and banana!" laughed Leila and Mum together.

"Well, I'm glad you enjoyed them," said Mum. "I've got plenty of bananas, so you can have marmite and banana sandwiches every day this week. OK?"

"Choice!" said Leila.

Weapons of Mass Description

Anna Kenna

The tall, thin, grey-haired doctor pursed his lips and shook his balding head. "I've examined your son, Mrs Adams," he said, "and I'm afraid this is one of the most serious cases I've seen."

My short, blond, green-eyed mother started to blub. The doctor passed her a soft, pastel-pink tissue from an oval, floral box on his large, brown, shiny wooden desk.

I wished I could stop this crazy word stuff. It had all started as a game. I didn't know that it would get so out of control that I'd end up having to fly miles to see this weird doctor about the problem.

It was our fair-haired, blue-eyed, freckly teacher's fault. We'd been learning about adjectives—you know, what they call describing words. Mr Fowles said that, for the rest of the day, we should practise using them and see how many we could come up with. Well, it got to be a bit of a competition between me and Shane. First I go, "Hey, short, curly-haired, skinny Maori friend. Can I borrow your new, green, torpedo-shaped rubber?"

"Sure, lanky, blond, straight-haired Pakeha mate," said Shane. "If I can use your scratched, white, plastic metric ruler."

We laughed our heads off. We thought we were so clever. Things kind of took off from there, and we ended up carrying on at lunchtime. I asked Shane what was in his lunch box.

"A soft, white-bread, crustless Marmite sandwich; a shiny, red, medium-sized apple; and a brown, sweet, oaty, home-made biscuit. What's in yours?"

Shane was good! I peered into my paper bag—I'd lost three lunch boxes, and Mum had said she wasn't going to buy me another one. "I've got a strawberry yoghurt in a red and white pot, a white-bread, sesame-topped roll with crisp lettuce, crunchy cucumber, and Mum's special creamy mayonnaise." I checked under the roll. "And a broken milk-chocolate biscuit."

It turned out even Stevens. We'd both used the same number of adjectives. But I was determined to beat Shane.

I got my chance later in our Maori class when Mrs Pene asked me to describe the Treaty of Waitangi. I couldn't help myself. I winked at Shane.

"Well, Mrs Pene, it's a very important, historic piece of fragile, stiff, yellowish paper that heaps of cloaked, tattooed Maori signed as well as Her Majesty Queen Victoria—the plumpish, rich, regal queen of England—

over how the green, lush, native lands of New Zealand were going to be ruled."

Everybody clapped. Mrs Pene's eyes were sort of crossed. She shook her head and turned another page of her notes.

By home time, Shane and I had had enough of all this adjectiving. But that's when the trouble started. We couldn't stop. I first noticed it at the shop when Shane was buying some lollies. I heard him say: "I'll have some of those chewy, creamy-white, milk-bottle-shaped ones and some red, dimply, hard-to-bite, raspberry-flavoured ones in the slightly dirty, left-hand metal tray."

"Cut it out, Shane!" I said. "I've had enough of that stuff."

He looked at me blankly. Then, when I got home, Mum asked how school was. I felt this lurch in my brain, and I said, "Oh, fun, a bit boring, hot, good, long, interesting, tiring . . ."

Mum looked at me as though I was really weird. I clamped my hand over my mouth and ran to my room. I didn't talk for the rest of the evening. When Mum and Dad asked why, I wrote a note saying that I was doing a sort of forty-hour famine, but it was with words instead of food.

The next morning when I woke up, I was just as bad. When Mum asked me what I wanted for breakfast, I said, "Some of those tiny, light-brown bubbles of puffed rice with full-cream cow's milk and a boomerang-shaped, ripe, yellow banana."

Mum kept me home from school for the rest of the week while she took me to see four doctors and a psychiatrist. Finally, we heard about someone who might be able to help—which is how we ended up here, in the Auckland office of Dr André Charles Wordsmitz, Specialist in Linguistic Addictions and Other Grammatical Diseases.

"He's already showing signs of tongue fatigue, and his vocal cords are under considerable strain," said Dr Wordsmitz, shining a bright light on the end of a long, slim, black, plastic tube down my throat. He whizzed across to a shelf and came back with this giant rubber brain with black lines and writing on it. I felt sick.

Dr Wordsmitz explained that brains contain little drawers full of words like nouns, verbs, and adjectives. "When we talk," he said, "these drawers open and shut as we choose the words we want. But sometimes," he said, drop-kicking the rubber brain into the rubbish basket, "a drawer gets stuck wide open. With this boy," he said, tapping me on the head, "it's the adjective drawer. It's become jammed through overuse."

"Oh, dear," wailed Mum, helping herself to another tissue. "What can we do?"

"Well, I have to say, Madam," said Dr Wordsmitz, suddenly becoming very pompous, "he should never have been playing around with adjectives in the first place. They are, after all, weapons of mass description, dangerous in the hands of children who don't respect them."

As Mum sobbed that it was all Mr Fowles' fault and that she was going to insist that our principal fire him, Dr Wordsmitz wrote down the treatment I was to follow. When we got home, Mum passed it on to Shane's mother.

The worst past was that we weren't allowed to talk at all for three days. Mum also had to take away the TV and all my books. As well, I had to rinse my vocal cords four times a day by gargling this foul purple stuff that made me want to throw up.

On day three, I was bored out of my brain and sitting at my desk making my forty-eighth model aeroplane when I heard a strange noise outside. I rushed to my window. I was just in time to see a big denim backside disappearing through our neighbours' kitchen window. Mum was in the garden, and I knew that if I shouted to her it would alert the burglar. I rushed to the phone and dialled 111—totally forgetting that I wasn't supposed to talk.

"Hurry," I said. "There's a burglar in our neighbours' house!"

The wail of the police siren must have startled the burglar because the next moment, I saw him shooting out of the Pollocks' front door and down the street. Two policemen leapt out of a squad car and tore after him.

How they didn't catch the dude I don't know, but five minutes later they came back, puffing like mad.

"He gave us the slip, sonny," said the older officer, wiping his forehead. "Thank goodness you saw him. Can you describe him for us?"

My heart was beating flat out. My mind was whirring. Mum came running over from the garden.

"He was . . . ah . . . um. He was . . . ah . . ." I tried to picture the burglar, but my mind was a total blank—zilch, zip, zero. I looked at the policeman with his pencil poised over his notebook. I really wanted to help, but just as I was about to open my mouth, I felt something in my brain slide shut.

"It's no good," I said, shaking my head. "I'm sorry, but I just can't describe him." Then I looked up at Mum and gave her this huge grin. "I can't find one single adjective to describe the burglar," I told her. "Isn't that fantastic? Not one measly, peasly word!"

The Violin

Gillian S. Findsen

When I first started learning, I hated the violin. It wasn't the lessons, or the practising. It was the violin, well actually the violin case.

When I was ten, my parents thought I should start having music lessons. We couldn't afford a piano—or fit one in our house. Mum heard from one of the neighbours that you could pick up new violins cheap. Not second-hand violins. For some reason the older they were, the more violins cost. And so I got a brand-new violin in a shiny black case.

I quite enjoyed the lessons after school. The problem was that I had to take the violin with me to school to get to my lesson on time. Once at school I could hide it under the teacher's desk but getting it to and from school was difficult. You see, I ride my bike to school. Dad rigged up a strap on the back of my bike but it didn't really work. I had to keep stopping to pull the blasted case back on again.

The other kids at school thought it was a real laugh. No one would ride with me any more 'cause I had to keep on stopping.

"There she is again," they'd jeer as they swooped past. "Putting her machine-gun case back on her bike!"

Sometimes I wished there was a machine gun! But whenever I checked there was always just the violin. It was embarrassing.

I took to carrying the case by the handle while I steered my bike with one hand. This worked OK on the sealed roads, but was trickier in loose metal—like on the road we lived down. If you got your wheel in the metal in the middle of the road you could fall off.

So one Tuesday afternoon I was riding home from my lesson, with my violin case swinging and banging against my legs, when it happened. The end of the case hit the front wheel and before you could say splat I was lying in the metal with my bike on top of me. The violin case, of course, had landed in the grass on the edge of the road. It was completely unharmed. I had blood trickling down both legs and one arm.

Mum was really sympathetic about the grazes—she cleaned them up and stuck plasters on. But she wouldn't let me give up the lessons. Nor would Dad.

"Not after all that money we spent on the lessons and the violin," they said. "Lucky it didn't get broken when you fell off your bike. Skin grows back."

The injustice of it.

The next day at school the kids had a field day when they heard what had happened. (Of course my rotten little brother told them.)

"Get shot up at your machine gun lesson?" they asked. "Enjoy your trip?"

"Concerto in B flat—flat on your face in the road!"

Ha, ha.

Next Tuesday I "forgot" the violin. Mum fumed up with it at lunchtime. Not so bad, I hadn't had to carry it on my bike. But the other kids thought it was great.

"Your Mum in the mob too, eh?"

That afternoon on my way home the violin tipped me off my bike again, this time as I was trying to straighten it behind me without getting off.

As I sat there with blood trickling from my knees and tears trickling from my eyes, I decided I had had enough. I swung the violin in its case hard onto the side of the road. It disappeared into the long grass under the neighbour's hedge.

Mum wasn't home when I got there so I cleaned up my knees myself. When she got home she asked how my lesson had gone.

"Fine," I answered. "I learnt a new piece." Oops!

"Come on then. Let me hear it while I peel the spuds."

"Oh, I don't feel like it just now . . . Maybe tomorrow."

I never could lie to my Mum. She reckons my eyes change colour when I tell lies. I think she just knows me too well.

"Where's the violin?" she asked.

"I . . . ah . . . I put it away . . ." She just stared. "I . . . ah . . . I lost it on the way home . . ."

"Well you'd better find it," she said quietly, going on peeling potatoes. "And do it quickly."

Mum's always more dangerous when she's quiet than when she yells. I found it. I played her my new piece.

"Very nice," she said at the end. "I can't see why you hate it so much."

So I told her why I hated it so much. I told her that I liked the violin and I liked the lessons, I just didn't like carrying the case!

All she said was "Uh-huh," and "Here, pass me a couple more carrots from the fridge."

But later on that evening, Mum said to me, "How about if I drop off your violin at the music teacher's house on Tuesdays and Dad can pick it up on Wednesdays, when he goes to the sales?"

"That'd be great Mum," I said with surprise. My parents aren't so bad after all. And maybe one day I'll be a famous musician!

A Load of Junk

John Lockyer

Mum likes doing up old furniture. Sometimes Dad and I help her. One day she started pulling stuff out of a corner in the garage. "I need more room for my furniture," she said. "Let's get rid of this junk."

"It's not junk," said Dad. "It's good stuff. It might come in handy one day."

Mum shook her head. "Come on," she said. "Let's load up the ute."

We loaded an old computer, some chipped flowerpots, a chair with three legs, a large purple lampshade, a pile of old newspapers, some rusty tins, four bent pram wheels, a split watering can, a bald tyre, a crate of old jars, a suitcase without a handle, and a twisted eggbeater. Mum threw two cracked plastic buckets onto the heap and then clapped the dust off her hands. "OK," she said. "That's a full load."

Dad tied everything down and then drove us to the dump.

The dump was busy. Some people were dropping stuff off, and others were picking it up. Dad parked the ute beside a large, tangled pile of bits and pieces. He pushed open the door. "Let's get our lot unloaded," he said.

Mum didn't move. She was staring at the pile of bits and pieces. I tapped her on the arm and pointed to Dad, who was untying the ropes.

"Right," she said, stepping out of the ute and getting a closer look at the pile of junk.

The dump was smelly, and there were bits of tin and glass lying around, so I stayed in the ute and looked through the back window. Dad worked hard, pulling junk off the ute. Mum worked hard too, loading junk onto the ute.

Dad unloaded the computer. Mum loaded a sky-blue vase with a chipped lip.

Dad unloaded the flowerpots and the watering can. Mum loaded a cast-iron coffee table.

Dad unloaded the chair. Mum loaded four tins of red paint.

Dad unloaded the lampshade and the newspapers. Mum loaded a cooling fan with bent blades.

Dad unloaded the tins and pram wheels. Mum loaded a pot plant.

Dad unloaded the tyre. Mum loaded a guitar with three strings.

Dad unloaded the jars. Mum loaded a roll of garden hose.

Dad unloaded the suitcase and the eggbeater. Mum loaded an oil painting of a blue lady.

"Hey!" Dad yelled when he saw that the pile on the ute wasn't getting any smaller. "I thought we came here to get rid of junk, not get more."

Mum's eyes sparkled. "It's not junk," she said. "It's good stuff. It might come in handy one day."

Dad slapped his forehead and groaned. Then he saw Mum smiling. He looked at me, and we both laughed.

Dad tied everything down. Then he drove us home . . . with another load of junk.

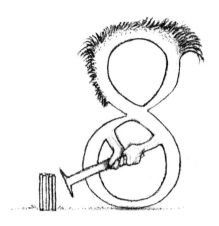

Horse

Adrienne Jansen

"You're in the team, Sam," said Mike the coach, after the practice.

Sam grinned. Now he would get to play in the cricket tournament.

"I'm in the team," he said to Bill and Jerome. They were in the team, too, and they had been in the team last year as well.

"Good one," said Jerome. "But just wait till you play against Horse."

"Who's Horse?" said Sam.

"Tell him about Horse, Bill," said Jerome.

"Horse," said Bill, "is this tall—" and he held his hand high above his head.

"He's got a bat that's so heavy no one else can use it," said Jerome.

"And he hits the ball so hard!" said Bill. "You don't want

to be around when he hits the ball."

"But who is he?" said Sam.

"He's a legend," said Jerome. "He's the biggest player in the Eastern Bays team."

"He's the biggest player in the tournament," said Bill.

"Is he bigger than Gareth?" Gareth was the biggest boy on their team.

"Way bigger," said Jerome. "Just you wait till you see him."

Sam wasn't in a hurry to see Horse. But he was looking forward to the tournament. He lay in bed at night and thought about how many runs he would get. He might get fifty! He could see himself getting the fiftieth run, and all the other boys shouting and clapping.

Every day after school he practised with Bill and Jerome, and every weekend they practised with their coach, Mike, and the rest of the team. And after every practice, when they walked home, they talked about Horse.

"Wait till he bowls to you, Sam. You won't even see the ball coming."

"You'll be dead if he bowls to you. Last year he bowled one to me that just about broke my bat."

"If you hadn't got your bat to it, it probably would have broken your leg!"

"Wonder if he'll be even faster this year?"

Sam lay in bed and thought about Horse. He imagined himself standing there with his bat and Horse bowling to him, the ball coming at him so fast he had to duck and the ball going wham! straight into the wickets. And Horse would grin, a big grin with lots of teeth.

Then Sam would be bowling to Horse, and Horse would swing that big bat of his and hit the ball right over the boundary for six.

"Do you know Horse?" he asked Mike next day.

"Horse?" said Mike. "Oh, you mean that boy in the Eastern Bays team. What have the others been telling you about him?"

"How big he is."

Mike laughed. "Don't worry about him. You'll be OK."

It was all very well for Mike to laugh. He didn't have to face Horse. Sam kept thinking about him.

Finally the tournament arrived. Sam's team played for three days. They won all their games. Finally, on the last day, as they were all piling into Mike's van to go to the grounds, Mike said, "Guess who we're playing today? Eastern Bays."

"Oh no!" said all the boys. "Not Horse! They'll kill us!"

Eastern Bays were going to bat first. Sam looked at their team. "Which one's Horse?" he asked Bill.

"The one with the cap on," said Bill.

Sam looked. He was a bit disappointed. Horse wasn't much taller than the others.

"He's not that big," he said.

"He looked bigger than that last year," said Bill. "But wait till he bats. He'll bat first."

But Horse didn't bat first. Or second. Or third. Their first four batsmen were out when Mike called, "Your turn to bowl, Sam." Sam took the ball, and looked to see the next batsman walk out.

It was Horse! He was going to bowl to Horse! Suddenly his knees felt shaky. He walked back, ready to bowl, polishing the ball on his pants. He looked at Horse. Horse was standing, bat ready, in front of the wickets.

Sam started to run in. He bowled as hard as he could, then waited for the ball to come flying back at him off Horse's big bat.

"Yeah, Sam!" "You've got him!" The other boys were all shouting, crowding round him, slapping him on the back.

"You've bowled him, Sam!"

Sam couldn't believe it. Horse had missed the ball. It had hit the wickets, and Horse was walking away. He had bowled Horse out with his first ball!

"Good on you, Sam!" said Mike after the game. "I told you not to worry about Horse. He's just big, that's all, and all you boys have grown a lot in the last year. You've caught up with him."

That night, Sam thought about bowling out Horse. He thought about each moment of it—the ball leaving his fingers, waiting for it to come back at him, the big shout from the others, and everyone crowding around. He thought about it over and over again.

And he thought about going to the tournament again next year. He could already hear what the other boys would say. "There's that boy that got Horse out last year. Is he fast! He's small, but he's so fast!"

"Remember when he bowled out Horse?"

"Yeah, first ball. Horse didn't even see it, it was so fast."

"What's his name?"

"Rocket. You'll be dead when he bowls to you. That kid Rocket—he's a legend!"

Uncle Trev and the
Howling Dog Service

Jack Lasenby

I woke and heard a dog howling across the farms out the back of Waharoa and, somewhere further off, so far away I could hardly hear it, another dog howled back.

"They're barking at the moon," my mother said next morning, but Uncle Trev had a different story when he dropped in for a cup of tea on his way home from the Wednesday stock sale at Matamata.

"They're not barking at the moon," he said. "Don't go telling your mother now, but they're trained howling dogs. Mine. I trained them myself years ago."

I looked at Uncle Trev and he looked back at me. "Years ago," he repeated, "I got sick of paying the post office for toll calls. It took ages to get through, then half the time you didn't get the person you wanted, and when you did you couldn't hear them for the noise on the line.

77

"I don't suppose you're old enough to remember," he said, "but people had much smaller ears before the telephone. They've only grown into these big flaps on the sides of our heads since we started squashing them with the telephone receiver." I heard Mum give a sniff from the bench where she was making a cup of tea. "Have a look in the album at the old family photographs, if you don't believe me," said Uncle Trev. "You can't even see ears on your grandmother.

"Besides," he said, "that old Mrs Eaves on the telephone exchange at the post office, she was always listening in. I could hear her breathing whenever I was talking to somebody. Sometimes, she'd even join in the conversation.

"I was lying awake one night, thinking about it," Uncle Trev went on, "and the dogs were barking across all the farms between my place and Waharoa, and I thought, "Those dogs are talking to each other!"

He stared at me. "That's when I got my idea!" he said.

I stared back at him. Mum put a cup of tea and a plate with a few slices of cake on the table. "Isn't it time you were in bed?" she told me.

Uncle Trev waited till she'd gone back to the bench. "A howling dog service," he said, "that was my idea! I remembered how we used dogs to carry messages in the trenches in the Great War, and how my mate Squeaker Tuner always said we should teach the dogs to talk.

"Well, it took me a few years, but I got hold of some expensive huntaway bitches and bred pups from them for their voices. They had to be able to bark high and clear so the messages would carry, and they had to be able to remember a long message, that was the other thing. I started selling my dogs cheap," said Uncle Trev, "and they were good working dogs too, so in no time I had them planted on farms from one end of the country to the other.

"From Waharoa on a clear night, a good howling dog can make himself heard in Matamata. From Matamata they howl the message up the Hinuera Valley, round through Cambridge to Hamilton, and up to Auckland. The reply comes back through Morrinsville and Walton to Waharoa before the first dog's finished rattling his chain. Of course," he said, "if the wind's from the north, they howl the message round the other way.

"You listen," said Uncle Trev, "and you'll hear them howling off messages in all directions, specially on a clear night. Auckland, Wellington, Christchurch, Dunedin — our howling dogs cover New Zealand."

"What about Cook Strait?" I asked.

"No trouble!" said Uncle Trev. "Sound travels good-oh across water. I'm even thinking of putting a dog on top of Mount Cook to howl messages to Australia."

"It's long past your bedtime," Mum said to me. "As for you," she said to Uncle Trev, "if you've finished your tea, isn't it time you were getting home to your farm? You've got cows to milk in the morning."

When he called in next week, I asked him how the dog was doing on top of Mount Cook.

"You wouldn't believe the trouble I'm having," said Uncle Trev. "It's so cold in the snow, the first dog I put up there got chilblains and wouldn't bark, so I'm crossing my best huntaway with a beardie collie to get a longer-coated dog. It's going to take a year or two to get a good pup though, and even then it's still got to be trained."

"How much do you charge for your howling dog services?" I asked him the next time he called in.

"It's cheaper than toll calls," said Uncle Trev. "You see, the dogs earn their tucker working in the daytime, and it costs me nothing to get them howling messages. There's nothing a dog likes more than to have a good old howl at night, specially if there's a moon.

"Actually, I've had a bit of trouble with the post office. They were really scared when they found my howling dog service had taken most of their business. They sent their Post-Master General in his uniform with red stripes down the trousers and a shiny brass helmet. I asked him if he was a fireman, but he got off his horse and begged me with tears in his eyes to stop the howling dog service. He said the post office was going broke."

Mum was banging some pots around on the bench. I didn't want her to hear Uncle Trev's story or she'd send him home. "What happened?" I asked.

"I felt a bit sorry for him," said Uncle Trev, "so I said I'd close down my howling dog service if the post office cut the cost of its toll calls in half. The Post-Master General couldn't thank me enough. He wanted to give me a free telephone, but I told him I didn't want big lugs instead of ears. I said I'd just go on using the howling dog service for myself and a few friends. I couldn't stop the dogs talking to each other, of course. They still howl dog messages all over New Zealand.

"The Post-Master General thanked me and put on his shiny brass helmet, jumped on his horse, and rode back to Wellington."

"Are you going to sit there talking nonsense all night?" said my mother. "Isn't it time you were getting home to the farm?" she asked Uncle Trev. "As for you," she said to me, "you're supposed to be ill in bed, not sitting up listening to a lot of silly stories."

I said goodnight and heard Uncle Trev's old lorry rattle away. It was warm under the blankets. I lifted the blind. Outside, it was frosty, and there was a moon. Somewhere down Ward Street, a dog howled. I listened, and out towards Uncle Trev's farm under the hills at the back of Waharoa, another dog replied.

Would You Like to be a Parrot?

Barbara Hill

> When Andrea went to the zoo,
> She looked at the parrot and said,
> "I wish I was just like you,
> All green and blue and red."

And when Andrea woke up next morning—she *was*! Her head was green, her front was red, and her back was bright blue.

"Oh, wow! I'm a parrot!" she said. When she put on her clothes, the colours came through. "Hurray! I'm a parrot!" she said.

Andrea floated down the stairs, and fluttered into the kitchen.

"I'm a parrot, I'm a parrot!" she cried.

"So you are," said Mum. "How did that happen?"

So Andrea said,

> "When I went to the zoo,
>
> I looked at the parrot and said,
>
> "I wish I was just like you,
>
> All green and blue and red."

And when I woke up this morning, I was like this."

"Oh dear," sighed Mum. "What do parrots eat for breakfast?"

"Birdseed!" said Dad, from behind the morning paper.

Mum gave her a banana, but Andrea decided parrots liked weetbix and toast and milk as well, because she was hungry.

"Don't forget to clean your teeth!" called Dad, as usual, when she left the table.

"Parrots don't have teeth!" laughed Andrea. (But she cleaned them just the same.)

Andrea flew off to school. She waved her arms, and twirled on her toes when people stared. She flapped into school, and flopped on the mat.

"Look at Andrea! Look at Andrea!" shouted the children.

"How beautiful you are," said Miss Mills. "How did it happen?"

So Andrea said,

> "When I went to the zoo,
>
> I looked at the parrot and said,
>
> "I wish I was just like you,
>
> All green and blue and red."

And when I woke up this morning, I was like this."

"You must have been at the zoo just at Wishing Time," said Miss Mills. "Look, children. Isn't Andrea lovely?"

"I wish I was pretty colours like that," sighed Sarah, and all the other children nodded, and wished that they were too.

Playtime, however, was not so good.

First she met the Headmaster, who said, "What's this? What's this! Go and wash that stuff off your face at once! The way some of you children come to school amazes me. Disgraceful! Disgraceful!" And he stamped off up the corridor.

Andrea knew it wouldn't wash off.

Outside was awkward too.

Children from other classes clustered round and rubbed her, to see if the colour would come off.

Ben Cook from Room 6 called her "Bird-brain", and Tom Riley yelled, "Bird-brain. Bird-brain. What a pain. Bird-brain."

That started others being smart.

"Green hair, green face.

Does she come from Outer Space?"
they chanted.

"Green face, green hair,

Nothing inside,—just Fresh Air!"

They rolled around laughing, they thought they were so clever, but Andrea ran inside crying.

"Never mind," said Miss Mills. "I still think you are beautiful. I know! I've got an idea! Let's have a Parrot Day!"

So the class stopped their usual work, and had a "Parrot Day". Everyone drew parrots, cut out parrots, read about parrots, and wrote stories about them. Everyone, that is, except Andrea! Parrots, of course, cannot read or write or draw, so Andrea didn't do those things . . . But parrots *can* talk, and Andrea talked and talked and talked. She had a wonderful time, flitting from group to group, and talking. Poor Miss Mills was quite glad when it was home-time.

After school, Andrea danced along the footpath, feeling very pleased with herself. When she came to the Pet Shop she poked her nose in and said, "I'm a parrot." Nobody took any notice, so she went right in. "I'm a parrot. I'm a parrot!" she said.

Mr Pitt, the Pet Shop owner, was talking to a tall man in flowing white clothes. An Arab. The Arab glanced at Andrea, and cried out in delight.

"So you are! So you are! A large South American Peticon Parrot, from the deepest, darkest jungle . . . And a talking one, too!"

He walked all round Andrea, and looked her up and down.

"An excellent specimen . . . Very rare . . . Very expensive . . . I must have. I buy! I buy! How much?"

"Hey," said Andrea. "I'm not for sale. And I'm not really a parrot. I'm a girl."

"You ARE a parrot," said the Arab. "Look at you. How can you be a girl?"

So Andrea said,

"When I went to the zoo,

I looked at the parrot and said,

"I wish I was just like you,

All green and blue and red."

And this morning, I woke up like this."

"There you are," said the man. "You *are* a parrot. You wished to be a parrot and you turned into a parrot. Very nice. Very rare. I buy! How much? Come on! How much?"

"I'm *not* for sale!" shouted Andrea. "I'm not for sale, and I'm not a parrot! I'm *not*! I'm NOT! I'm NOT!" And she *ran*. Out of the shop, over the road, round the corner and down the street. All the way home, as fast as she could go.

"Don't cry," said Mum. "Parrots don't cry."

"I'm not a parrot," sobbed Andrea. "I don't want to be a parrot. How can I stop being a parrot?"

"I don't know," sighed Mum. "I'd rather have my Andrea than a parrot. I wonder if it will wash off, if we rub really hard."

So Andrea sat in the bath, and soaked and soaped, and Mum scrubbed, and by the time Dad came home, her head was a paler green, her front was a pinky red, and her back was a soft pale blue. But she still looked like a parrot.

"It started at the zoo," said Dad. "Let's go back there."

So back they went, and,

> When Andrea got to the zoo,
> She looked at the parrot and said,
> "I wish I was *not* like you,
> *not* green, *or* blue, *or* red!"

And when she woke up next morning, she looked in the mirror and shouted,

"Hurray! I'm *me* again. Good!"

86

21

The Caves in the Cliff

Patricia Irene Johnson

Kathryn and her family lived in a little town on the edge of Tewaewae Bay, right at the bottom of the South Island. Her two brothers Mark, who was eleven years old and the boss, and Nick, two years younger and a born follower, always called her Katz. Kathryn at a mere eight years, didn't like it much, but she didn't let on.

She followed wherever they led—up the bush which hung like a heavy grey-green backdrop to the little town or down on the beach. The beach was Kathryn's favourite place. They played on this beach summer and winter. But for Kathryn summer was best, because you could swim in the sea and then lie on the hot sand to dry out and then swim again and again.

There was only one thing Kathryn didn't like about the beach—one thing that scared her. At the very back where the sand was always dry, there were high cliffs of yellow clay with brush growing here and there. One day Mark discovered that there were caves in these cliffs. Of course he wanted to explore them to find out where they led, and now quite often when they were playing on the beach Kathryn never knew when the boys were going to decide to go exploring.

Of course she didn't have to go with them, but she always felt it would be better to be with them than to wait on the beach worrying about them.

Kathryn was playing in the shallows when the call came.

"Hey Katz! We're going into the caves. You don't have to come if you don't want to."

They always said this and it was always followed by giggles. They knew she would follow them, but Kathryn knew that this was not so silly because at the end of the opening passage the cave branched out in several directions, each successive cave branching out again.

She often wondered if, once lost they would ever be found, because no one knew they played there. Did anyone know that there were caves in these cliffs anyway?

After clambering up behind them to the mouth of the cave Kathryn stopped irresolutely to glance back at the sea. Thrusting one hand into the pocket of her shorts she began nervously kneading a ball of wool her mother had given her earlier in the day. It was at that moment that she felt a pang of real fear, but of that fear an idea was born.

"Hurry up Katz!" called Mark. "We're going in right now."

"Coming," she called back, but instead of going inside the cave she bent down to tie one end of the ball of wool to a sturdy bush close by. Then she climbed into the cave.

Once in she turned for a last glimpse of the sea as it gently ebbed and flowed over the rippling sand ribs in the sunlight. Then she turned to stare into the twilight just inside the entrance. The roar of the sea was now reduced to a muffled murmur and while the floor of the cave felt cool to her hot feet, the air had a strange smell about it. Small as she was she had to bend over a little as she walked.

"What on earth are you doing, Katz?" yelled Mark in exasperation.

"I'm in! I'm in!" Kathryn yelled back angrily, muttering to herself about the impatience of boys.

As they crept forward, first into one cave and then from it into another, Kathryn realised that they had never moved so far into the cliff before.

"I'm not going any farther," she called finally. "We'll all get lost."

"Then you'll just have to wait here until we get back," yelled Mark. There were hoots of laughter from ahead of her and then the boys' voices slowly began to grow fainter and fainter as they moved farther into the caves.

Kathryn sat down on the floor and closed her eyes. She prefered her own darkness to the gloom of the caves. It wasn't so scary for one thing. If only she could hear the sea, but there was nothing—just silence. She leaned back against the wall of the cave and recited her favourite poems to herself until, without realising it, she fell asleep.

Kathryn woke suddenly, surprised to find herself in semi-darkness. Standing up quickly she hit her head on the roof of the cave then, as she gasped, she thought she heard a faint call. There it was again far away in the distance, but from somewhere deeper in the caves.

"Coo-ee!" she replied in the way Mark had taught them after he had read that this was the call used in the Australian bush.

She heard another call the same as hers. It was the boys all right. Ha! They'd got themselves lost after all. As loudly as she could Kathryn kept on calling and listening. It seemed forever before they reached her.

"So you did get lost after all," she crowed. "I knew you would one day."

"Let's get out into the sun," said Mark pushing past her. "I'm frozen."

"Well, you won't get out going that way," said Kathryn pushing in front of him.

"Since when have you been the one with the sense of direction?" snapped Nick.

"Since this afternoon," replied Kathryn. "You two lost your way today—remember?"

The boys were silent as they followed her back to the mouth of the cave.

Kathryn watched the little half-moon shape of light growing larger and larger until they were there. The roar of the sea seemed to fill the whole beach as she crawled out.

Laughing with relief, the boys raced past her down the cliff to the sand. Then, leaning to one side, Kathryn untied the wool from the bush, stuffing the ball back into her pocket. This would be her secret forever. What a pity Hansel and Gretel hadn't had a ball of wool to unwind as they walked through the forest. They would have found their way home quite easily.

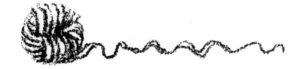

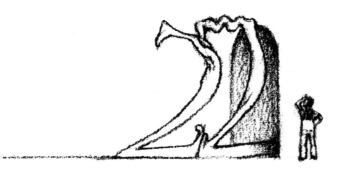

The Chocolate Bomb

Stuart Payne

It was a hot, hot summer. Eloise was on holiday. Each day her Auntie May gave Trevor some money to buy himself, Jane and Eloise ice creams. But at the shop, Trevor bought only ice blocks.

"Why can't we have ice creams?" asked Jane on the third day. "You could at least treat Eloise."

"The amount of cash at my disposal," Trevor replied pompously, "is not equal to the cost of the said frozen refreshments."

"Why does he talk like that," Eloise asked her cousin when the two of them were alone.

"Oh, he thinks he's a young adult," answered Jane. "And he thinks that the way to show it is to use big words when he talks."

"Ice blocks are OK," said Eloise, "but just once I'd like a chocolate bomb ice cream. Just once."

"Actually," said Jane, "I don't believe Trevor when he says he hasn't enough money for three ice creams. I think he's pocketing the extra money himself."

On the fourth day, the shopkeeper said he was almost out of ice blocks. But he assured them that there was no panic. The refrigerator truck was due tomorrow with fresh supplies.

The next day on their way down to the shop, Jane insisted they show Eloise the road tunnel which passed underneath the railway line. Jane called it the fairy tunnel.

"That's not its appellation," said Trevor haughtily.

"Its what?" asked Eloise.

"Its name, stupid," said Trevor. "It's not called the fairy tunnel."

"It is so," said Jane. "If you stand in the tunnel and make a wish when a train passes above, then your wish will come true. Let's wait for one to come."

"Simple superstition," mocked Trevor. "I'm not waiting, and if you're not in the shop when I buy the ice blocks then you won't get one."

"I'm going to wait," said Eloise. "I want to make a wish."

"I warn you, Eloise," Trevor said, "that this is but a figment of Jane's gullible imagination."

"When's the next train?" asked Jane.

"Not for hours," replied Trevor walking off.

"You're a spoilsport," called Jane.

"I'd like to make a wish," said Eloise, "but there's no point standing here for hours."

"I'll bet we won't have to wait for hours," said Jane, "Trevor just made that up. I've noticed that whenever he lies, he tries to talk big."

The girls remained as Trevor continued on to the shop and it was not long before they heard a train coming. Clickety clack, clickety clack, closer, closer.

"Wait till it's right overhead," called Jane.

Then with a rapid rat-a-rat-a-rat-a-rat-a the train rumbled above them.

"I wish for a . . ." called Eloise. But the noise was so loud Jane couldn't hear what she was saying.

"Come on, we better catch up with Trevor now."

"I don't think my wish will come true," said Eloise as they hurried to the shop. "Not as long as Trevor has the ice-cream money."

"You have to have faith, "said Jane. "Faith in the magic of the tunnel."

When they got to the shop, Trevor was just coming out.

"There are no ice blocks," he said. "The shop has run out." The girls didn't believe him; they thought that Trevor just didn't want to buy them any.

"We're going to tell Mum you're a stinge," said Jane.

"Check with the shopkeeper, then," Trevor retorted.

And indeed the shopkeeper confirmed it—he had run out. The supply truck, however, was due any minute. What's more it was a new one, bigger and better. But Trevor refused to wait. He wandered off.

"Well, leave us our share of the money," Jane called after him.

"No," said Trevor. "Mum said I'm responsible for it," and with that he disappeared around the corner.

Without any money it was no use Jane and Eloise waiting. Sadly they too started to wander off when a man ran up to the shop. It was the driver of the new ice-cream truck. He had tried to drive through the tunnel under the rail bridge but his new truck was too big. It had jammed there and damaged the refrigerator motor. If he didn't get everything out of it, all the ice cream would melt.

"We need everyone we can to help," the shopkeeper announced. He shouted to passersby to come and help. Soon a human chain was formed from the truck to the shop. Cartons of ice cream and ice blocks were unloaded from the truck and passed one by one along the chain and into the shop. Right in the middle of the chain were Jane and Eloise.

At last all the ice cream was saved. As a special reward all those who had helped were allowed a free ice cream of their choice.

"I know what I'm going to choose," said Eloise. "My wish has come true."

Later as the two girls walked leisurely home, Jane eating a jellytip ice cream and Eloise with a chocolate bomb, they met Trevor.

"Hey," he said. "How did you two get those?"

"Don't you mean how did we acquire these frozen refreshments," Jane replied.

"Don't get smart with me," Trevor demanded.

"These," said Eloise, swallowing a bite of her chocolate bomb, "are the enchanting figments of superstitious and gullible imaginations."

"That's right," added Jane. "Pure magic." And the pair of them walked on without giving Trevor a second glance.

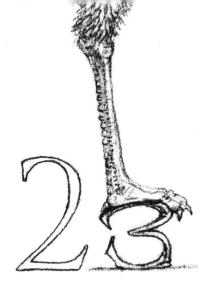

Ms Winsley and the Pirate Who Didn't Have a Problem

Barbara Else

Ms Winsley tightened the straps of her bright red togs. "Holidays are great," she said. "I am longing for a swim."

She waved to the parrots in the palm trees, called "Lovely weather!" to the kangaroos and ran down to test the water with her toe.

A very small person in a big black hat rowed a dinghy to the shore, climbed out and gazed around.

"Bother, bother, darn it," said the person.

"I am not here to work," said Ms Winsley to herself. She took one step into the water.

"It's not fair!" cried the person.

"I am here to have a holiday," Ms Winsley muttered firmly.

The person heaved a sorrowful sigh and made a choking sound. Ms Winsley could tell he would burst into tears any moment. She tried hard to take no notice. She tried incredibly hard. But it was no good, none at all.

"Excuse me," Ms Winsley said. "But do you have a problem?"

The person's lip trembled under his ginger moustache. Sure enough, a tear trickled down beneath the patch on his left eye. "No," he said. "Oh no. It's not a problem for a pirate, if he doesn't have a parrot."

"You're a pirate?" asked Ms Winsley.

"Call me Quentin," said the pirate.

"Cool," Ms Winsley said. "You rove the seven seas and shout out, *Yo-ho-ho!* Then you search for desert isles where you bury treasure chests chock-a-block with precious jewels!"

"And none of us have problems," Quentin said. "Never." He hid his face behind his big black hat. Ms Winsley heard a sob.

"I run Tricky Situation Services," she said. "I'm a consultant. I specialise in fixing problems." She squinched her toes up in the water, and whistled.

The pirate buried his face further in his hat.

"I'm very good at problems," said Ms Winsley. "Not that I'm boasting."

Quentin pulled his hat down to his chest and peered at her over the brim.

"Oh, go on," said Ms Winsley.

"It's like this," Quentin said. "All the other blokes had parrots. All but me. So I bought a really big one, very cheap.

It was going to sit on my shoulder like all the other parrots do. It was going to squawk *Polly wants a cracker*." He hid his face behind his hat again. "But it wouldn't. And it couldn't. And I really loved my parrot even so. But it ran off."

"You mean it flew off," said Ms Winsley. "Parrots fly."

"This one ran," repeated the pirate. "So here I am with nothing. Nothing but my broken heart." Another tear ran down his cheek. "But of course that's not a problem for a pirate." He dabbed his eyes on his hat brim.

"Of course not," said Ms Winsley. "But what say we pretend?"

"Oh, I don't mind pretending," Quentin said, and looked at her expectantly.

Ms Winsley set to work. She thought hard. Where would a parrot run to? It might try to find another parrot for some fun and games. Parrots are pretty big on fun and games.

Ms Winsley thought very hard. Waves frothed up the beach and down again. The parrots in the palm trees fluttered from frond to frond. "Have you checked that lot back there?" Ms Winsley asked.

The pirate sucked his ginger moustache. "I never thought," he said.

So Ms Winsley encouraged the pirate to come along the path under the palm trees. The vines curled darkly and the teeth of wild cats glimmered in the shadows. Quentin gripped Ms Winsley's hand. She decided he was very timid for a pirate, as well as very small.

The parrots clung to the tree trunks and squawked.

"Well?" Ms Winsley asked.

"None of those is mine," the pirate said. "My parrot's not as colourful as them. She's a whole lot bigger, too."

Ms Winsley looked at the parrots on the tree trunks. She looked at the hummingbirds. She looked at a large blue swan that wandered by.

She saw two skinny tree trunks just beside the path. As she looked, one of the skinny tree trunks took a step.

Ms Winsley realised that it was not a tree trunk. It was a leg — the leg of a very large bird. And the other little tree trunk was the very large bird's other leg.

"Cool!" exclaimed Ms Winsley. "An emu in the wild."

Quentin peered around her. "Ms Winsley, you're terrific!" he cried. "There she is! My parrot. You found Polly."

"But that's an emu," said Ms Winsley.

The pirate stroked the emu's feathers. "An emu? I suppose that's why she doesn't fly. I wondered why I got her cheap."

The emu lowered its long neck and nudged the pirate's earring. Though Quentin seemed a little happier, a tear still shone on his moustache.

"Any more problems we can pretend about?" Ms Winsley asked.

"Not really," Quentin said. His lower lip trembled again. "It must be because she's an emu that she won't sit on my shoulder, that's all."

Ms Winsley looked at the very small pirate. She looked at the very large bird. She clenched her jaw tightly to help her wrestle with the problem.

"Sometimes it's fine to be different from everyone else," Ms Winsley said at last. "Right?"

"That's why I became a pirate in the first place," Quentin said.

"So Polly can't perch on your shoulder. But you could sit on hers," Ms Winsley said.

Quentin's mouth dropped open beneath his ginger moustache. So Ms Winsley gave him a leg-up and there he was, a pirate sitting neatly on the emu's back.

"Terrific!" he said. "And it doesn't really matter that she won't say she wants a cracker. Two things out of three's not bad. It's not a problem. Truly."

"But if it's all right to be different," said Ms Winsley, "and you're sitting on her shoulder, you can be the one to call out *Polly wants a cracker*."

The pirate's eyes shone like diamonds. "And I can shout my *Yo-ho-ho!* whenever I get off. Ms Winsley, how can I thank you?"

"Just be nice to your pet, and help me if I need it," said Ms Winsley. "Though next time you find a treasure chest, perhaps you could remember me. Remember me a lot."

"Polly wants a cracker!" Quentin shouted. Polly raced over to the dinghy with the pirate on her back. They climbed in and the pirate rowed away.

"It's very satisfying to help people out of tricky situations," said Ms Winsley to the parrots in the palm trees.

"Polly wants a cracker!" squawked the parrots. "*Awk!* Polly wants a cracker." And the kangaroos played kickball while Ms Winsley had her swim at last, in the warm and deep blue sea.

Intruders

Elizabeth Best

Willie turned the spare key in the lock and pushed open the door of the flat. He wasn't supposed to call in at home after school. He was supposed to go straight to Mrs Vinchey's and wait there for Mum to pick him up after work. But today his bag was really heavy, and he was superhungry. He threw his gear down in the hall and went into the kitchen to look for a biscuit. He'd hardly got started in the pantry when the doorbell rang.

"G'day, kid," said a big man when Willie opened the door. "Your mum home?"

"No," said Willie and then wished he hadn't. Mum's warnings about what to say when you answered the door or the telephone were ringing in his ears.

"She's right, mate," the man shouted over his shoulder to an invisible person outside. Then he pushed the door open wide, just as if Willie wasn't there, and waddled down

101

the hall to the living room. Willie followed and stood in the doorway looking at him. Mum always said not to let anyone into the flat unless you knew them very well. But Willie hadn't had a choice.

The man pulled a metal tape out of his pocket and began measuring the windows. Willie wondered whether he was a burglar measuring the place so that he could break in one dark night. But he didn't need to break in—he was already inside.

The doorbell rang again. This time a skinny, scruffy man with a beard and dirty trousers pushed open the front door.

"Where's the boss?" he asked.

"In here, mate," shouted the man in the living room, and for the second time that afternoon, a stranger pushed past Willie.

"I'm not supposed to let . . ." began Willie. Then he stopped. He wanted to tell the men to go away, but he wasn't sure how to do it. If only Margie from next door were home, he'd go and get her—but she didn't finish at the library until four o'clock.

In the living room, the skinny man began writing on a notepad. "Fifty-sixish, fifty-sevenish," he said, the words muffled through his beard.

"Who *are* you?" asked Willie.

"Eh?" said both men together.

"Who ARE you?" asked Willie, a little louder this time.

"Stan," replied the man with the tape-measure. "Stan's your man." He roared with laughter, and the rolls of fat under his T-shirt wobbled like jelly.

"What are you doing here?" Willie asked.

But Stan had had enough socialising for one day. He went back to measuring the windows—and the doorbell rang again.

"Right!" thought Willie. "This time I won't let anyone else in." But it was too late. A third man was already walking down the hall just as the first two had done. That was when Willie remembered that he'd left the key in the door. Another mistake.

"Hi, there," said the man as he went by.

Willie didn't reply. He was acting calm on the outside, but inside, he was beginning to feel very strange. He could just hear Mum saying: "Why did you come home in the first place? And why did you let all those strangers into our home?" He wished he'd done what he was supposed to and gone straight to Mrs Vinchey's. He wondered if he should run to her place right now. But that would mean leaving the men in the flat with no one to watch them.

The man who'd come in last was banging on the living room wall with his fist. Willie decided to try again.

"What are you all doing here?" he called out.

"Aha!" said Stan. "That's for us to know and for you to find out." He rocked with laughter, and all his jelly rolls rocked with him.

At last Willie had an idea. He went into the kitchen and telephoned his friend Joseph.

"Do you think I should ring the police?" he whispered into the telephone after telling Joseph what was going on.

"Not yet," said Joseph. "I'll come round and check things out first."

Joseph must have run all the way because, in a few minutes, Willie heard him coming up the path. It felt a whole lot better having a friend with him, but it didn't make any difference to the men. They were in a huddle on the floor now, talking and looking at figures.

"You're right," said Joseph when he and Willie were alone in the kitchen. "This *is* a job for the police. Come on, we'll phone them from my place."

Willie nodded, but just as he and Joseph were about to leave, the skinny man with the beard walked along the hall and out of the flat. The man who'd come in last followed him, and the front door slammed shut.

Willie and Joseph looked at each other. Was Stan going to leave, too? Perhaps all their troubles were over. Then they heard a strange, shush-shushing sound.

They raced to the door of the living room and looked in. Stan wasn't sitting on the floor any more. He was standing beside the far wall, sharpening a scraping tool. As they watched, he put the sharpening stone in his pocket and reached up to the wall with the scraper.

"Stop!" yelled Willie.

"Police!" shouted Joseph.

Stan got such a fright that he spun round. The scraper went shooting out of his hand and across the carpet. Willie dived on it.

"Throw it here," called Joseph.

"Hey! That's enough, you kids. Give that thing back!"

"*What* is going on here?" demanded a voice from the doorway.

Mum was standing in the living room. She looked furious.

"Willie! Mrs Vinchey rang me at work. She's worried sick about where you are." She looked at Stan. "And what are *you* doing in my flat?" she asked.

"Will you ask your boys to give me back my scraper?" said Stan, annoyed. "Remember, you're paying me by the hour."

"I'm not paying you anything," said Mum.

Stan's face turned bright red, and now someone else was coming into the flat.

"Yoo-hoo! Anyone home?" It was Margie from next door. "I don't suppose anyone's seen some workers from Arthur's paint and paper place?" she asked. "They were supposed to start on our walls at three-fifteen, and they haven't shown up."

"Uh, oh," said Joseph and Stan at the same time. Mum groaned—and suddenly Willie saw the chance to get himself out of trouble for not going straight round to Mrs Vinchey's.

"Heck, Mum," he said, trying to look serious and relieved at the same time. "Just think, if I hadn't been here this afternoon, the new wallpaper we put up last month would be torn to shreds by now." For a split second, he thought he had Mum convinced. Then she looked at him—hard.

"Hold it right there, Willie," she said, so calmly that it was worrying. "If you'd gone to Mrs Vinchey's after school like you were supposed to, we'd never have had this problem in the first place."

"You have to admit," said Stan, scratching his head, "she sure has got a point there."

Why Anna Hung Upside Down

Margaret Mahy

One day Anna, wearing her blue jeans, went out and climbed onto the first branch of the second tree to the right of the supermarket.

Then she hung by her knees.

She saw the world upside down. The grass was the sky and the sky was the grass. The supermarket poured people upward into the green air.

An old man with a ridiculous hat came by.

"Look at this girl," he said to a thin woman with fluffy slippers and curlers. "She's upside down."

"My goodness so she is!" the thin woman cried. "Why do you think that's happened?"

"I don't know," the man replied. "Perhaps it's the weather. We've had some funny weather lately, and it may be affecting the children."

"Perhaps she's doing it for health reasons," said a

sickly-looking goat. "Being upside down lets the blood into the brain, and that perks you up no end."

A lion and a school inspector going home from the supermarket stopped to look on curiously. The lion said nothing, but the school inspector said, "It's the parents' fault. Parents let their children do anything these days. Now this poor child's parents are most likely at home drinking tea and reading the paper and not looking after their girl. *They* don't care that she's gone all upside down out here."

"Yes, that's right!" called the mother of twins. "They don't care at all. Now if my twins were to go all upside down like that, I'd smack them with the hair brush. That'd bring them right way up again pretty quick, I can tell you."

At this point, a boy called Ron, oldest of five, climbed up into the tree too and hung beside Anna.

"Look at that, now there's two of them at it," cried an excited voice, probably a hen. There were quite a few hens in the crowd.

"It's catching, it's catching," shouted the thin woman in fluffy slippers, and the crowd moved back several steps nervously.

"I don't want to go upside down," whimpered a rich man. "All my money would fall out of my pockets."

"Neither you shall!" said his pretty secretary, hurrying him away and looking angrily at Anna and Ron as she went.

"It's the new craze," said a folk-singing crocodile strumming on her guitar. Then she sang, showing long rows of well-kept teeth:

"Upside down—upside down—

The newest craze to hit the town . . ."

But at this point a little girl called Sally, wearing a tracksuit, climbed into the tree and hung by her knees next to Ron.

"I still say it's the weather!" cried the man in the ridiculous hat.

"Now then," said a policeman coming up. "What's all this?"

"Look, look, the police have come," twittered some excitable guinea pigs, and a small number of culprits and criminals slunk away to evade the eye of the law.

"These poor children, neglected by their parents, have gone all upside down," said the School Inspector in an important voice.

"But perhaps," suggested a Professor of Philosophy going by with a meat pie in a paper bag, "perhaps they are the right way up. Perhaps it is we who are upside down."

This upset a lot of people. There was a resentful muttering and the sound of gritting teeth.

The policeman had to do something quickly. People and animals were all upset. He thought hard.

"Send for the fire brigade," he commanded at last.

But the lion, who had been watching thoughtfully, said in a deep lion's voice, "Ask them! Ask them why they are hanging upside down."

The policeman came up to Anna. "Now then, young lady!" he said, "why are you upside down in that tree?"

"I learned to do this yesterday," replied Anna, "I just wanted to see if I could still do it today."

"It's fun!" shouted Ron. "You all look funny upside down."

And Sally shouted, "Upside down, frowns turn into smiles."

Then Anna put up her hands and swung down from the branch, and so did Ron and Sally.

"Why are you doing that?" asked the man in the ridiculous hat.

"Well, the bend of my knees is starting to hurt a bit," Anna said. "And not only that, it's dinner time and hanging upside down makes you hungry. Are you coming?" And then all three walked away, leaving the first branch of the second tree to the right of the supermarket absolutely empty.

Beans

Patricia Grace

Every Saturday morning in the winter term I bike into town to play rugby. Winter's a great time. We live five kilometres out of town and the way in is mostly uphill, so I need to get a good early start to be in town by nine.

On the way in I don't get a chance to look around me or notice things very much because the going is fairly hard. Now and again where it gets a bit steep I have to stand on the pedals and really tread hard.

But it's great getting off to rugby on a Saturday morning with my towel and change of clothes on the carrier, and pushing hard to get there by nine. It's great.

By the time I get to the grounds I'm really puffing and I know my face is about the colour of the clubhouse roof. But I'm ready to go on though. I can't wait to get on the field and get stuck into the game; I really go for it. I watch the ball and chase it all over the place. Where the ball goes

I go. I tackle, handle, kick, run, everything. I do everything I can think of and I feel good.

Sometimes it's cold and muddy and when I get thrown down into the mud and come up all mucky I feel great, because all the mud shows that I've really made a game of it. The dirtier I get the better I like it because I don't want to miss out on anything.

Then after the game I strip off and get under the shower in the clubroom, and sometimes the water is boiling hot and sometimes as cold as anything. And whatever it is, you're hopping up and down and getting clean, and yelling out to your mates about the game saying is it hot or cold in your one.

I need a drink then. I get a drink from the dairy across the road and the dairy's always jammed full of us boys getting drinks. You should hear the noise, you should really hear it.

The going home is one of the best parts of all. I hop on my bike and away I go, hardly pushing at all. Gee it's good. I can look about me and see everything growing. Cabbages and caulis, potatoes and all sorts of vegetables. And some of the paddocks are all ploughed up and have rows of green just showing through. All neat and tidy, and not much different to look at from the coloured squares of knitting my sister does for girl guides.

You see all sorts of people out in the gardens working on big machines or walking along the rows weeding and hoeing: that's the sort of place it is around here. Everything grows and big trucks take all the stuff away, then it starts all over again.

111

But I must tell you. Past all the gardens about two kilometres from where I live there's this fairly steep rise. It's about the steepest part of the way home and I really have to puff up that bit. Then I get to the top and there's a long steep slope going down. It's so steep and straight it makes you want to yell and I usually do. That's not all though.

Just as you start picking up speed on the down slope you get this whiff of pigs. Poo. Pigs. It makes you want to laugh and shout it's such a stink.

And as I go whizzing down the stretch on my bike I do a big sniff up, a great big sniff, and get a full load of the smell of pigs. It's such a horrible great stink that I don't know how to describe it.

We've got a book in our library at school and in it there's a poem about bells and the poem says "joyous". "The joyous ringing of bells" or "bells ringing joyously". Something like that. Well "joyous" is the word I think of when I smell the pigs. Joyous. A joyous big stink of pigs. It's really great.

It's not far to my place after I've taken the straight. When I get home I lean my bike up against the shed and I feel really hot and done for. I don't go straight inside though. Instead I flop myself down on the grass underneath the lemon tree and I pick a lemon and take a huge bite of it.

The lemons on our tree are as sour as sour, but I take a big bite because I feel so good. It makes me pull awful faces and roll over and over in the grass, but I keep on taking big bites until the lemon is all gone, skin and everything. Then I pick another lemon and eat that all up too because I don't want to miss a thing in my life.

We have an old lady living next door to us. She's pretty old and doesn't do much except walk around her garden. One day I heard her say to Mum, "He's full of beans that boy of yours. Full of beans."

When Mum Won Lotto

Valerie Batchelor

Mum got a Lotto ticket for her birthday.

So on Saturday night, everyone watched the numbers.

"3, 16, 23, 31, 26, 40, and the bonus number is 7," said the Lotto man.

"Hooray!" said Mum. "I've won Lotto."

"Have you won first prize?" asked Harry.

"Can we get a beach house?" asked Keri.

"And a boat?" asked Harry.

"Woof!" said Jess.

"We didn't win first prize," said Mum. "We haven't won enough for that."

"Can we get a new car?" asked Keri.

"And a motorbike for Dad?" asked Harry.

"Woof!" said Jess.

"No," said Mum. "We haven't won enough for that."

"Can we get a TV in my bedroom?" asked Keri.

"And a stereo for me?" asked Harry.

"Woof!" said Jess.

"No," said Mum. "We haven't won enough for that."

"Can I have a mountain bike?" asked Keri.

"Me, too," said Harry.

"Woof!" said Jess.

"No," said Mum. "We didn't win enough for that."

"Let's buy heaps of party food," said Keri.

"Chocolate," said Harry.

"Woof! Woof!" said Jess.

"Biscuits and fizzy drink," said Keri.

"Well," said Mum, "I think we might have won enough for that. If it's a fine day tomorrow, we'll buy some biscuits and some chocolate and some fizzy drink, and we'll have a picnic in the park."

And it was. So they did. And Jess came, too.

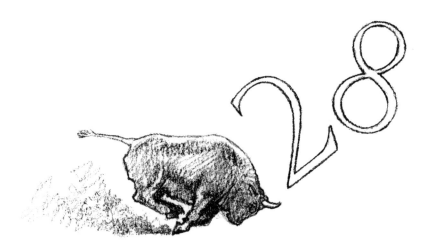

Sebastian

Janice Leitch

We were staying with Uncle Barney when he bought the bull. We didn't know it was a bull at first. Uncle Barney had me on.

"The name's Buttercup," he said. "You're the youngest, you milk her."

I wasn't fooled for long. But when I tried the same trick on Melanie, she said: "And you go collect the rooster's eggs."

We climbed up to the top paddock to see the bull. Just before the paddock was a huge open concrete water tank set into the ground.

"Want to go through the bull paddock?" I asked.

"No way!" Melanie shuddered, and for once I agreed with my sister.

The bull was huge! He was huge and black! He was huge, black and very angry. He pawed at the ground.

"You'd snort if they called you Buttercup," said Melanie.

"That's not his name," I said. "Uncle Barney was having you on. It's Sebastian Sylvester O'Sullivan."

"Huh?" said Melanie.

"He was on TV in England. Want his autograph?"

"If you get it for me."

Sebastian snorted.

"Don't be scared," called Uncle Barney, who was in the paddock. "He's timid, you can pat him."

Timid? We weren't going to pat him. Sebastian turned when he heard Uncle Barney. Sebastian got bigger and blacker. He started running. So did Uncle Barney.

Uncle Barney reached the fence, and jumped over. Sebastian went straight through the fence and splashed down in the water tank.

When we got there, Uncle Barney was brushing himself down. But Sebastian was stuck.

Uncle Barney took his hat off. "Hmm," he said. "Hmm, heavy bull, not sure how we'll rescue him."

First he got the tractor and a rope. Uncle Barney got in the tank to tie the rope round Sebastian's chest. "Let's hope it works," he said.

But as the tractor backed away from the tank, the rope broke, Sebastian fell back in, and we were drenched by the wave that surged over the side.

"Go and phone Davey," said Uncle Barney. Davey's his neighbour, and if anyone would know how to get a bull out of a tank, he would.

"Hold your horses," said Davey. "I'll be right over."

117

"Some animal you have there, Barney," laughed Davey when he saw Sebastian. "Shame you let him hop in the tank, won't be easy to get him out."

"Sebastian's having a whale of a time," giggled Melanie.

"Some new sort of fish," I laughed.

"It's no time for jokes," said Uncle Barney.

"Got it!" said Davey. "Get a crane and winch the bull out."

Uncle Barney slapped Davey on the back. "That's it!" he said. "A crane. Could cost a bit, but no matter."

When the crane arrived, the driver laughed and laughed. "Nice one, Barney, I've never seen the likes of this before."

"The skin on his fingers will be wrinkled," whispered Melanie. I thought of my own hands after a bath. Do bulls have fingers? Rats, she caught me again.

This time Uncle Barney put a chain round Sebastian's chest. Uncle Barney and I fixed the fence so Sebastian could be lifted up, swung over the fence and into his paddock. At least, that was the idea.

We cheered as the bull rose out of the water. We cheered as the crane swung towards the paddock. Then we screamed and leapt out of the way when the chain broke.

We thought the bull would be furious, but Sebastian didn't worry about revenge. He charged straight through the fence and into his paddock.

Sebastian never escaped again. But he got bigger and blacker and meaner. And he snorted like a steam engine whenever he saw Melanie, Uncle Barney or me!

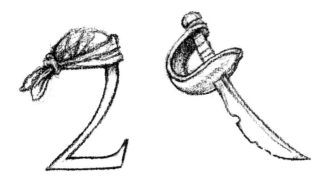

Just One Thing

K.E. Anderson

Mrs Funnell is famous for telling stories. She's the best storyteller in the whole school.

On Monday, Mrs Funnell was telling a story about how she used to be a pirate captain before she was a schoolteacher. She had her old pirate scarf on and her pirate eyepatch, and she held a treasure map in her hand. Out of her pocket poked the handle of a pirate pistol. It was made from gold and silver and was covered with red and green and blue jewels.

"Just then," said Mrs Funnell, "a cannon ball crashed right through the bow of my ship, and we started to sink. My crew were so terrified that they all jumped overboard into the shark-infested water. It was a terrible sight. I grabbed my spyglass and peered out over the ocean. Not too far away, I saw a tiny island, so I rushed to my cabin. The boat was sinking fast, so I only had time to put one thing in my pocket before I jumped into the longboat and rowed to the island. With this one thing, I knew I was sure to be rescued."

"What was it?" asked Blair.

"Would anyone like to guess?" asked Mrs Funnell. "Ellen?"

"Some matches so you could start a fire to attract attention?"

"Good guess," said Mrs Funnell, "but no, I didn't take any matches with me."

"A mirror so you could reflect the sun off it and get the attention of passing ships?" suggested Blair.

Mrs Funnell smiled. "Good thinking, but no, I didn't take a mirror with me."

"Did you take your spyglass and use the glass to make a fire to signal with?" asked Tracey.

"Hey," said Mrs Funnell, "you would all make amazing pirates. But no, I lost my spyglass overboard as I jumped into the longboat."

Suddenly Colin had an idea. "Did you quickly write a message while you were in your cabin, put it in a bottle, and throw it into the sea?"

"Great idea, Colin, but no, I didn't put a message in a bottle."

The class had run out of ideas.

"Would you like me to tell you what I took with me?" asked Mrs Funnell.

The whole class nodded.

"My cellphone," said Mrs Funnell, taking it out of her pocket. "All I had to do was push 111, and I was rescued at once by the coastguard."

On Tuesday, when the children arrived at school, Mrs Funnell was wearing her astronaut suit . . .

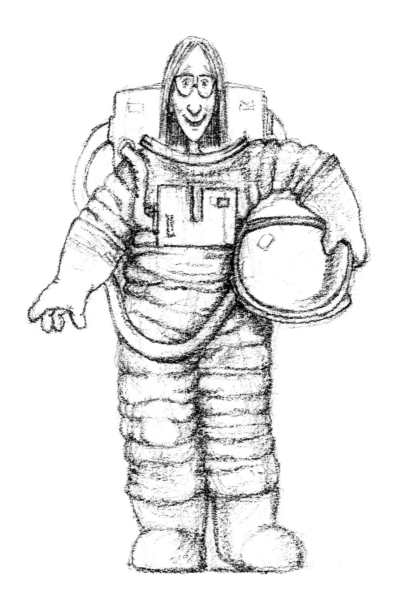

Where's Pete?

Penelope Newman

The bell rang, and everyone sat down.

Mrs Spicer looked around.

"Where's Pete?" she asked.

"Oh, I think I saw him being kidnapped by wild bears this morning," said Nicola. "They were planning a picnic, and they wanted him to come too."

"Is that right?" said Mrs Spicer, smiling.

"Oh, I just remembered. I think I saw him setting off to climb Mount Everest this morning," said Andrew. "He probably won't be back till at least lunchtime."

"Really?" said Mrs Spicer.

"No, no, I'm sure I saw him waving from the window of an alien spaceship," said Hiria. "He seemed to be having a good time, anyway."

"Oh yes?" said Mrs Spicer.

"Well, he told me he was going on a balloon trip round Africa today," said Briar. "I hope he took his sandwiches— it's a really long way!"

"How interesting," said Mrs Spicer.

"I heard he was off to the Himalayas," said Tom. "He wants to catch a blue speckled snurk. They're very rare."

"OK," said Mrs Spicer with a grin. "Does anybody *really* know where Pete is?"

"All right, then," said Lily. "He's still playing with Gavin, out there in the playground."

Mrs Spicer sighed with relief. "Oh, good. And who's Gavin?"

"Oh," said Lily. "Just his pet dinosaur."

Index

Anderson, K.E.   'Just One Thing'   119

Ashton, Christine   'Mayday!'   45

Batchelor, Valerie   'When Mum Won Lotto'   114

Best, Elizabeth   'Intruders'   101

Buxton, Jane   'Leila's Lunch'   57

Cowley, Joy   'The Reading Room'   9

Else, Barbara   'Ms Winsley and the Pirate
                        Who Didn't Have a Problem'   96

Findsen, Gillian S.   'The Violin'   66

Grace, Patricia   'Beans'   110

Hill, Barbara   'Would You Like to be a Parrot?'   82

Hill, David   'Silent Reading'   21

Hudson, Rose   'Pavlova Queen'   11

Jansen, Adrienne   'Horse'   73

Johnson,
    Patricia Irene   'The Caves in the Cliff'   87

Kenna, Anna   'Parent Help?'   52

                        'Weapons of Mass Description'   60

Lasenby, Jack   'Uncle Trev and the Light Bulb'   28

                        'Uncle Trev and the Howling Dog Service'   77

Leitch, Janice   'Sebastian'   116

Lockyer, John   'A Load of Junk'   70

Mahy, Margaret   'Green Marmalade to You'   50

                        'Why Anna Hung Upside Down'   106

Newman, Penelope   'Where's Pete?'   122

Noonan, Diana   'Circus Routine'   33

Payne, Stuart   'The Chocolate Bomb'   92

Schroder, Margaret   'The Case of the Phantom Tagger'   42

Sidney, Karen   'Witches Britches'   17

Slater Bottin, Janet   'Trapped by an Octopus'   14

Smith, Miriam   'Roimata and the Forest of Tane'   38

Todd Maguire,
    Cynthia   'The Super-Trolley'   24

[ANSWER to *The Case of the Phantom Tagger:*
It was Luke. He couldn't have been reading a book called
Surfing in Switzerland. Switzerland is a land-locked country.]